I0796598

lonely planet KIDS

THE BUGS BOOK

ACKNOWLEDGMENTS

Editorial and Design by Imago Create

Author: Nancy Dickmann
Illustrator: Bethany Lord/Advocate Art Agency
Consultants: Dr. Alberto Zilli and Dr. Nick Crumpton
Publishing Director: Piers Pickard
Publisher: Rebecca Hunt
Editorial Director: Joe Fullman
Editor: Katie Dicker
Art Director: Andy Mansfield
Designer: Dan Prescott, Couper Street Type Co.
Print Production: Nigel Longuet
Proofreader: Nicola Edwards
Americanization: Kris Hirschmann

Published in October 2025 by Lonely Planet Global Ltd

CRN: 554153
ISBN: 978-1-83758-675-2
www.lonelyplanet.com/kids

Printed in Malaysia
10 9 8 7 6 5 4 3 2 1

STAY IN TOUCH
lonelyplanet.com/contact

Lonely Planet Office:
IRELAND
Digital Depot, Roe Lane (off Thomas St),
Digital Hub, Dublin 8, D08 TCV4

THE BUGS BOOK

NANCY DICKMANN

Consultants
Dr. Alberto Zilli and Dr. Nick Crumpton

Illustrated by
Bethany Lord

CONTENTS

A WORLD OF BUGS

We often think that humans rule planet Earth. We build giant cities and travel all over the world. But did you know there's a secret army living all around us, mostly out of sight? There are more bugs alive right now than all the humans who have ever lived. In fact, for each person alive right now, there are more than a billion bugs! They're divided into millions of different species—each one equally fascinating.

PREHISTORIC BUGS

Insects and other creepy-crawlies have been around for a very, very long time. The first species evolved more than 400 million years ago, long before the dinosaurs appeared. Some of these prehistoric bugs were able to fly, making them the first flying animals. One species, *Meganeuropsis permiana*, looked a bit like a supersized dragonfly, with a wingspan of 28 inches (71 cm).

This artwork shows the scale of *Meganeuropsis permiana*, which was about four times wider than the largest living dragonfly today!

Some bugs create spectacular homes—from giant termite mounds to the delicate hexagonal cells of a honeybee hive, shown here.

SURVIVING AND THRIVING

Bugs can survive almost anywhere. There are bugs living in the freezing polar regions, in hot, dry deserts, in high mountain regions...even in water! Bugs are a hugely diverse group of animals, and each species has evolved features and behaviors that help it to survive in its environment. For example, some bugs have coloring that helps them to blend in with their background and hide from predators. Other bugs are poisonous, or have a venomous sting. Many bugs can fly, while others spin webs to trap prey to eat.

Can you spot the leaf insect here? Its body looks almost exactly like a leaf.

WE NEED BUGS!

If you've ever been stung by a wasp or had ants ruin a picnic, you might see bugs as little more than pests. And it's true that some species cause problems for humans, such as by damaging crops or spreading disease. But we should also celebrate the lives of these tiny creatures. Many pollinate plants so we can grow crops. They provide food for other animals, and they break down the bodies of dead animals and plants, which makes our soil rich. The simple truth is bugs are amazing! And we must learn to share our planet with them.

Bugs are full of protein and can provide food for us too! These fried larvae are being sold in a market in Cambodia.

BUGS UNDER THREAT

There's no doubt that bugs are important, but something more alarming is equally true—bugs are under threat. Scientists have discovered that populations are dropping all over the world, and many species are disappearing entirely. Studies show the overall number of insects on Earth, for example, is going down by 1–2 percent every year. Farming and the construction of buildings destroy habitats, and climate change makes it harder for bugs to survive. We need to take steps if we want to protect the world's bugs.

Electric lights, such as this floodlight, can attract and confuse bugs. They may lose their way or be easier for predators to spot.

WHAT'S IN A NAME?

Bugs, minibeasts, creepy-crawlies—you'll hear these tiny creatures described by different names. But what do they all mean, and how are they different? This book covers a wide range of creatures from different animal groups, including insects, arachnids, and myriapods. But no matter how different they may look, they all belong to a much larger group called arthropods.

Woodlice (see page 80) such as the one shown here, are part of an arthropod group called crustaceans. This group also includes crabs and lobsters. Woodlice are the only crustaceans that live their lives entirely on land.

WHAT'S AN ARTHROPOD?

Arthropods are the largest group of animals on Earth—over 80 percent of all animal species belong to this group! Instead of having a skeleton inside their body, like we do, arthropods have a hard outer exoskeleton that protects the softer parts inside. When they outgrow it, they shed it to reveal a new one underneath (see page 12). Their body is divided into segments, with legs arranged in pairs. These legs are made up of several stiff pieces that can be moved thanks to soft joints between them. The name "arthropod" comes from Greek words referring to these jointed limbs—*arthro* (joint) and *pod* (foot).

Arthropods use their jointed legs to crawl and clamber across terrain. These ants are using their legs to work together to form a bridge.

INCREDIBLE INSECTS

Insects form the largest branch of the arthropod group. All adult insects have a body that is divided into three parts: the head, thorax, and abdomen. There are three pairs of legs attached to the thorax. Insects have a pair of antennae on their head, which helps them to sense the world around them. Insects use their antennae to touch, but they also use them to smell, by picking up chemical signals in the air.

Most insects have two pairs of wings, like this dragonfly, but there are plenty of species that have just one pair or none at all.

AMAZING ARACHNIDS

Spiders, scorpions, and ticks belong to a different group from insects: the arachnids. Arachnids have a body that is divided into two parts: a cephalothorax and abdomen, though in some groups of arachnids the two parts are fused together. Arachnids have four pairs of legs, rather than three like insects. They also have two further pairs of appendages—pedipalps and chelicerae—which are used mainly for feeding or defense.

Pedipalps

Chelicerae

In arachnids, the pedipalps are feelers or pincers, while the chelicerae are jaws or fangs.

MARVELOUS MYRIAPODS

Myriapods, which include centipedes and millipedes, take their name from the Greek words *myria* (10,000) and *pod* (foot) meaning "10,000 feet." While these animals do have many pairs of legs, no species has yet been found with quite that many! Myriapods have long, caterpillar-like bodies divided into segments. Centipedes have one pair of legs on each segment, while the segments of millipedes have fused together in pairs to look like two pairs of legs per segment. Centipedes can have anywhere from 15 to 177 pairs of legs, while the leggiest millipede ever discovered has 653 pairs!

This Tanzanian blue ringleg centipede is looking after her young, seen here in white. Even the juvenile centipedes have lots of legs!

A BUG OR NOT A BUG?

So what exactly is a bug, then? Sometimes this word is used to refer to bacteria, viruses, or other tiny living things that can cause illnesses such as colds. The word is also a general term that covers various minibeasts, such as the insects, arachnids, and myriapods in this book. But just to make things more complicated, there is also a subgroup of insects known as "true bugs." They have special mouthparts adapted for sucking sap from plants. One example is a leafhopper (see page 31).

CLASSIFYING BUGS

Scientists divide bugs into large groups called classes—these include insects, arachnids, and myriapods. They then divide these classes even further, putting them into groups, called orders, of closely related species. Members of each subgroup might live in different parts of the world, but they share similar characteristics, such as body structure. Let's take a look at some of the most common orders.

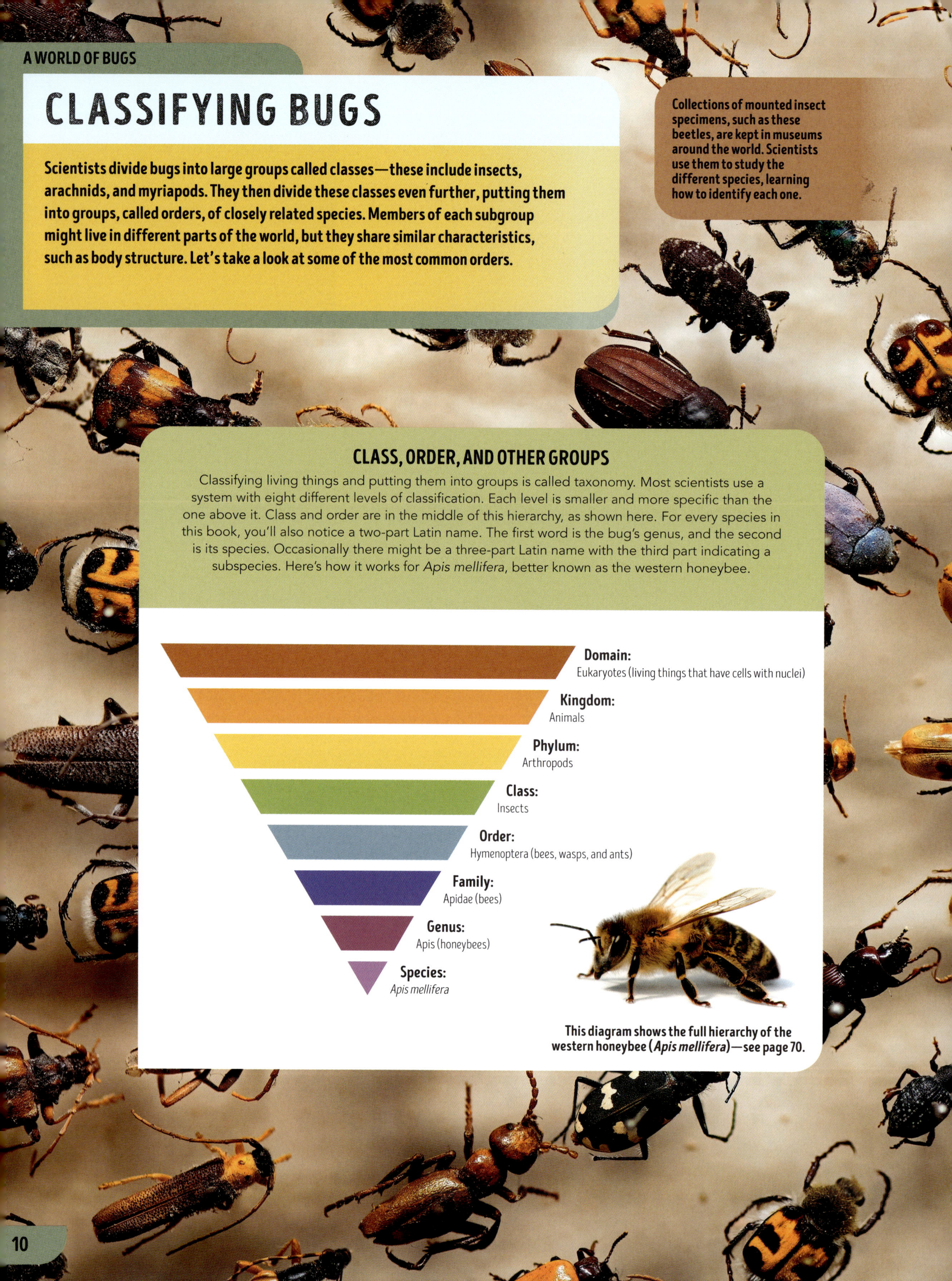

Collections of mounted insect specimens, such as these beetles, are kept in museums around the world. Scientists use them to study the different species, learning how to identify each one.

CLASS, ORDER, AND OTHER GROUPS

Classifying living things and putting them into groups is called taxonomy. Most scientists use a system with eight different levels of classification. Each level is smaller and more specific than the one above it. Class and order are in the middle of this hierarchy, as shown here. For every species in this book, you'll also notice a two-part Latin name. The first word is the bug's genus, and the second is its species. Occasionally there might be a three-part Latin name with the third part indicating a subspecies. Here's how it works for *Apis mellifera*, better known as the western honeybee.

This diagram shows the full hierarchy of the western honeybee (*Apis mellifera*)—see page 70.

ARACHNID ORDERS

Spiders are probably the most well known of the orders that make up the arachnids. Ticks and mites make up another order called Acari, and an order called Opiliones includes the spiderlike harvestmen (see page 36). Scorpions make up their own order, and there are also separate orders for similar-looking creatures known as vinegaroons or whip scorpions, as well as for tiny pseudoscorpions (see page 21).

Vinegaroons are a type of arachnid. They get their common name from the vinegar-like acid they squirt when they feel threatened.

INSECT ORDERS

There are many different orders of insects. Butterflies and moths are grouped together in the order Lepidoptera ("scaly winged"). Diptera ("two wings") is the order that flies, mosquitoes, and some other two-winged insects belong to. Ants, bees, and wasps make up the order Hymenoptera ("membrane-winged"). Grasshoppers and crickets form their own order, Orthoptera ("straight wings"), and cockroaches and termites form another, Blattodea (from the Latin word *blatta*—an insect that shuns the light). There are also many smaller groups. Earwigs, for example, make up the order Dermaptera ("skin wings").

Earwigs have pincers and their leathery forewings protect their hindwings, like a skin. They make up a small order, with only about 2,000 species in 12 families.

AND THE WINNER IS...

The largest order of insects is called Coleoptera, better known as beetles. There are about 400,000 different species in this group. That means around 40 percent of all insect species—and 25 percent of animals overall—are beetles. That's a lot! Most beetles have two sets of wings. The hindwings are soft and flexible, and beetles flap them to fly. The forewings are hard coverings, called elytra, that protect the hindwings.

To fly, a ladybug (see page 64) lifts its hard, spotted forewings to reveal the translucent flying hindwings hidden underneath.

A BUG'S LIFE

Have you seen photos of yourself as a baby? You might think you look a lot different now. You're bigger, of course, but your body parts are much the same. That's just how humans grow! However, growing up can look quite different in other parts of the animal kingdom. Many arthropods have life cycles in which the young look completely different from the adults.

GETTING BIGGER

For arthropods, an exoskeleton is a great way to stay safe—it's basically like wearing a suit of armor. However, the exoskeleton can't grow. When an arthropod gets too big for its outer covering, a new, soft exoskeleton begins to grow beneath it. The outer exoskeleton splits and the creature wriggles out. Over the next days and weeks, the new exoskeleton will harden. This process is called molting. Some arthropods molt just a few times, while others shed their exoskeletons dozens of times during their life.

After a molt, an arthropod leaves its old exoskeleton behind. It looks like a hollow copy of the creature's body, as seen with this dragonfly.

METAMORPHOSIS

Insects' bodies change in a process called metamorphosis. In some species, the young that hatch out from the eggs look similar to their parents, although it takes time for their wing cases to develop. Known as nymphs, these types of juveniles molt and grow until they are adults. Each stage between molts is called an instar. In other species, the young are called larvae, and they look completely different from the parents. After a number of molts, they reach a form called a pupa. A pupa may create a covering called a chrysalis or cocoon to protect its body as it changes into its adult form. This is how caterpillars turn into butterflies and moths.

The butterfly life cycle has four main stages, moving from egg to caterpillar to pupa to butterfly. The pupa creates a chrysalis as a form of protection during metamorphosis.

ARACHNID LIFE CYCLES

Unlike insects, arachnids do not go through an obvious metamorphosis. The young that hatch from spider eggs are called spiderlings, and they look similar to their parents. They grow and molt until they're adults. Ticks start as six-legged larvae before molting into eight-legged nymphs. The nymphs eventually molt into an adult form, which looks similar but is capable of producing young.

Unlike most other arachnids, scorpions do not lay eggs. They give birth to live young, which ride on the mother's back.

Butterflies are the final stage of a long and complicated life cycle. This common Jezebel (*Delias eucharis*) is found in many parts of Asia.

MYRIAPOD CHANGES

Myriapods, such as centipedes and millipedes, lay eggs. The young that hatch out have the same basic body shape as adults. However, in most species their bodies have fewer segments—and therefore, fewer legs. At each molt they add body segments and legs until they reach their adult size.

Some centipede species have all their body segments and legs when they hatch, such as this juvenile Tanzanian blue ringleg centipede (see page 9).

NORTH AMERICA

North America is the third-largest continent, stretching from the icy polar regions nearly all the way down to the Equator. Its rugged mountains, vast plains, and thick forests provide a range of different habitats for insects and other creepy-crawlies. Wherever you look, it's a safe bet there's a species of bug that's adapted to thrive here!

In the far north, many different flies have developed ways to survive months of freezing temperatures.

In the high Rocky Mountains, it is cool and the air is thinner, but many bugs, such as bees, can survive here.

The hot desert regions have fewer plants, but hunters, like spiders and scorpions, find a way to live here.

Vast forests in the east are home to many bugs, from beetles and flies to moths and mosquitoes.

MAP KEY

- Polar Ice
- Arctic Tundra
- Evergreen Forest
- Temperate Forest
- Tropical Forest
- Temperate Grassland
- Shrubland
- Desert
- Wetlands
- Mountains

The vast grasslands of the prairies are a perfect place for bush crickets, beetles, and butterflies.

Tropical rainforests in the far south form a warm, moist environment for ants, butterflies, and dragonflies.

RED VELVET ANT

Don't be fooled by the name—the red velvet ant isn't an ant at all! It's actually a type of wasp with thick red hair on its body, which makes it look like a big, furry ant. Female red velvet ants are slightly larger than the males, and they don't have wings, which makes the resemblance to ants even stronger.

FACT FILE

- **Scientific name:** *Dasymutilla occidentalis*
- **Class:** insect
- **Length:** up to 1 in (2.5 cm)
- **Home:** fields, meadows, and other sunny, warm areas with sandy soil
- **Diet:** larvae eat the larvae of other insects; adults eat nectar from plants

HANDLE WITH CARE

The bright color of a red velvet ant's body is a warning to predators. It shows that the velvet ant is dangerous and not worth trying to eat. These wasps also make a squeaking noise to scare off predators. Any that don't take the hint are in for a nasty shock! Red velvet ants have a tough exoskeleton that is hard to bite through. The females are also armed with a stinger laced with powerful venom.

Male red velvet ants don't sting, but they can fly away from danger. They are less brightly colored than the females.

Female red velvet ants can't fly. These solitary creatures are found crawling on vegetation or scurrying on the ground.

DANGEROUS YOUNG

Red velvet ants are a type of parasite that kills their host. The females spend much of their time looking for nests built on the ground by other wasp species. When they find one, they creep inside and lay their own eggs on the larvae that are already there. Once the eggs hatch, the red velvet ant larvae eat the other wasp larvae. They remain in the host nest, eating more and more of the larvae until they pupate and emerge as adults.

Red velvet ants often seek out the nests of the eastern cicada killer wasp, shown here, to lay their eggs.

SPINY-BACKED ORB-WEAVER

The beautiful spiral webs that you see sparkling with dew in your garden are likely the work of an orb-weaver spider. Members of the orb-weaver family are found all over the world, but this odd-looking spiny-backed orb-weaver is most commonly seen in the southern United States, from California to Florida. The female spiders have a yellow or white abdomen with black spots, ringed with six sharp spines that can be either red or black.

FACT FILE

- **Scientific name:** *Gasteracantha cancriformis*
- **Class:** arachnid
- **Length:** up to 0.5 in (1.3 cm) wide (though males are smaller)
- **Home:** woodlands, shrubby gardens, and citrus groves
- **Diet:** insects

CATCHING PREY

Spiny-backed orb-weavers use their webs to catch prey. A female spins a new web each night. These webs are delicate and beautiful, but they're deadly traps for any passing small insects. The spider waits at the center of the web until she feels the vibrations of an insect landing on it and getting stuck to the sticky silk. She wraps the insect in more silk so it can't escape and uses her fangs to inject venom to paralyze it. Then she uses her mouthparts to break through the insect's exoskeleton, discharge digestive fluids, and suck out the gooey insides.

This spiny-backed orb-weaver, seen from underneath, has sucked out the gooey insides of her trapped prey.

GROWING UP ALONE

When it's time to mate, a male spiny-backed orb-weaver finds a female's web and dangles nearby on a strand of silk. Then it taps on the web, using a distinctive rhythm that the female recognizes. Once the male has approached, the female uses her own silk to strap him down. The male dies after mating, and once the female has laid her eggs in a special egg sac, she dies too. When the eggs hatch, the tiny spiderlings must make their own way in the world.

Female spiny-backed orb-weavers can fit on a fingernail, as shown by this closely related Asian species: *Thelacantha brevispina*. The males lack spines and are even smaller and less colorful.

This spider's species name translates from Greek and Latin to mean "belly thorn crab shape," and it's not hard to see why!

EASTERN DOBSONFLY

Go for a walk near a stream in the eastern United States and you're likely to see a dobsonfly flitting around. With their large size, twin pairs of wide wings, and long, pointed mandibles—or jaws—these insects really create an impression. But this insect species has a secret! It lives a double life—adults fly through the air and breathe air, but their larvae live and hunt underwater.

FACT FILE

- **Scientific name:** *Corydalus cornutus*
- **Class:** insect
- **Length:** larvae are up to 3.5 in (9 cm); adults are slightly smaller
- **Home:** near rivers and streams in the eastern United States
- **Diet:** larvae eat insects, worms, and molluscs; adult females eat nectar; adult males do not feed

LIFE IN THE WATER

The eastern dobsonfly lays its eggs close to the edge of a stream or river, on overhanging rocks or branches. Once the eggs hatch, the larvae (called "hellgrammites") fall or crawl into the flowing water. There they live on the bottom, crawling over rocks and sand as they hunt for prey. They feed on any small creatures they can catch, including the larvae of other insects. As they grow, they molt, shedding their exoskeleton to reveal a new, bigger one underneath. They may molt up to a dozen times before they're ready to become adults.

Dobsonfly larvae look nothing like their parents. It can take up to five years for a larva to reach its adult form.

ADULT FLIES

Adult dobsonflies have a short lifespan—just three days for males, and around 10 days for females. The male and female adults look fairly similar, with wide heads, long antennae, even longer abdomens, and translucent, veined wings. When they're not flying, the wings are folded over their back. However, there is one feature that makes the males and females very easy to tell apart. The females have sharp, curved mouthparts called mandibles. But male dobsonflies have mandibles that are much, much longer. During their short lives, the males don't feed but use their mandibles for fighting rivals.

The mandibles of a male eastern dobsonfly can be half the length of its body.

Eastern dobsonflies, like this female, have a brown, mottled appearance. This becomes a useful camouflage against tree trunks or muddy soil.

HICKORY HORNED DEVIL

Most people would agree that this caterpillar looks like something out of a horror film. The hickory horned devil is one of the largest caterpillars in North America, with a scary-sounding name and orange spikes to match, but it's actually harmless! (Unless you're a leaf, that is...) These huge caterpillars eventually turn into big moths that look completely different, but equally cool.

FACT FILE

- **Scientific name:** *Citheronia regalis*
- **Class:** insect
- **Length:** larvae up to 5.5 in (14 cm); adults have a wingspan up to 6 in (15.5 cm)
- **Home:** deciduous forests of the eastern United States
- **Diet:** larvae eat leaves; adults do not feed

Hickory horned devils have big appetites. A single caterpillar can strip a whole branch of its leaves!

MULTIPLE MOLTS

The hickory horned devil is the caterpillar of a moth known as the regal moth. Regal moths lay their eggs in the summer on the leaves of trees, particularly nut trees such as walnut and hickory. The eggs hatch about a week later, and the tiny larvae that crawl out are yellow. As they grow, they molt four times. With each molt, their appearance changes, and it's only after the fourth and final molt that they take on the bright green form with orange horns.

The spikes on the caterpillar's head do not sting, but they scare off birds and other predators.

TIME FOR A CHANGE

When fall comes, it's time for the caterpillar to move on. It crawls down the tree, digs into the soil on the forest floor, and forms a case around itself to protect it as its body changes shape for the last time. The pupa stays underground during the winter months, then the adult moth emerges the following summer. The moths immediately start to look for a mate, and then the females begin laying eggs. The moths do not eat and only live for about a week.

The regal moth has an orange body, with wings of grayish-green with reddish-orange veins and pale yellow spots.

DEER TICK

Some bugs feed on plants, while others hunt prey to eat. Ticks are a little different. They are parasites that attach themselves to host animals and drink their blood. They don't want to kill their host—if they did, there would be no more blood! Deer ticks, also known as black-legged ticks, live in any part of North America where their favorite host animal—deer—are found.

FACT FILE

- **Scientific name:** *Ixodes scapularis*
- **Class:** arachnid
- **Length:** up to 0.1 in (3 mm)
- **Home:** on animal hosts, mainly in wooded areas of eastern North America
- **Diet:** blood

BLOODSUCKERS

Deer tick eggs hatch into tiny larvae in the summer. The larvae wait on the tips of grasses or shrubs for a host animal, such as a mouse, to brush past. They latch onto a host animal as soon as they can find one, and after they feed, they drop off. Later they molt into nymphs and repeat the feeding cycle before molting again into their adult form. Deer ticks use their special mouthparts to pierce the host's skin, then insert a feeding tube that keeps them anchored in place. As they feed, their body swells with blood.

While adult ticks and nymphs have eight legs, like spiders, larvae (shown here) have only six legs, but they are still arachnids.

Ticks can't fly or jump. They grasp onto greenery while they wait for a host, and outstretch their front legs, ready to hitch a ride.

CAUSING HARM

Deer ticks often bite people, but they don't take enough blood to affect a person's blood supply. However, they can carry and pass on different diseases to humans when they bite them. One of the most common is Lyme disease, caused by a bacterium called *Borrelia*. Deer ticks pick up *Borrelia* bacteria when they feed on infected animals, such as mice. Lyme disease can cause fever, headaches, and tiredness, and its symptoms can last for months or even years.

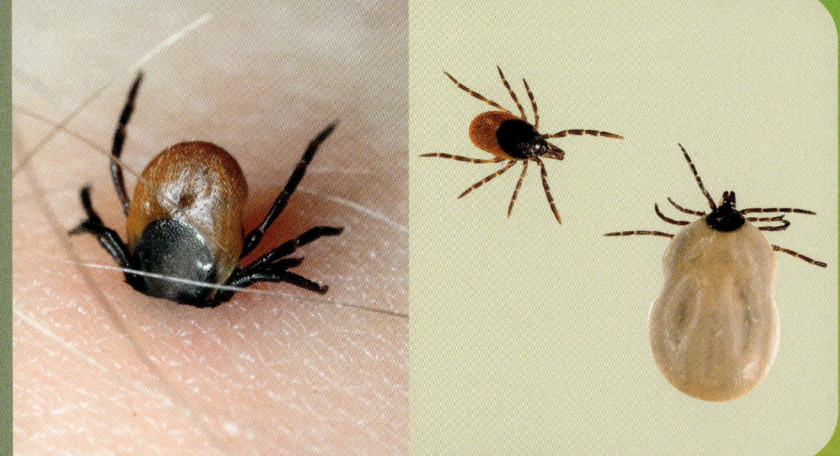

A deer tick buries its head firmly into the skin to feed (left) and can swell to several times its original size after feasting on blood (right).

GREEN STINK BUG

Also known as the green soldier bug, this shield-shaped insect is a common sight in the gardens of eastern North America during the summer. They're called "stink bugs" because their bodies have glands that spray out a smelly liquid to ward off predators, much like a skunk does. Some people describe their scent as smelling like a combination of coriander and burned rubber. Ugh!

FACT FILE

- **Scientific name:** *Chinavia hilaris*
- **Class:** insect
- **Length:** up to 0.8 in (2 cm)
- **Home:** orchards, woodlands, and crop fields of eastern North America
- **Diet:** juices from plants and fruit

YOUNG LIFE

In the summer, adult stink bugs lay their eggs in clusters on the underside of a leaf. They choose a plant that will provide food for the young stink bugs once they hatch about a week later. Green stink bugs often choose fruit trees or vegetable plants, such as peas or corn. As the nymph feeds and grows bigger, it molts several times. Stink bugs are mainly black when they hatch, but their appearance gradually changes with each molt. It will take about five weeks for the nymph to become an adult.

These young black and green stink bugs have been through three molts.

Adult stink bugs are almost as wide as they are long—about the size of a small paperclip.

CROP PEST

Like many of their relatives, green stink bugs have a special mouthpart, called a proboscis, for piercing plants and sucking out their juices. As they feed, they inject special chemicals into their food that make it runnier and easier to suck. These chemicals, plus the loss of their juices, damage the fruits and other plants that the stink bugs feed on. Because they often feed on food crops, such as fruit trees or vegetables, they are considered a pest by farmers.

The green stink bug uses its long, needle-like proboscis to feed on the seeds, stems, and leaves of plants.

HOUSE PSEUDOSCORPION

Scorpions can be deadly, with big pincers to grab their prey and a stinger at the end of the tail to deliver a dose of venom. Luckily, the house pseudoscorpion is not dangerous! The clue is the "pseudo" part of the name, which means "not real"—these tiny creatures might look a bit like scorpions, but they are a different group entirely.

FACT FILE

- **Scientific name:** *Chelifer cancroides*
- **Class:** arachnid
- **Length:** up to 0.2 in (5 mm)
- **Home:** leaf litter, tree bark, and sometimes buildings
- **Diet:** smaller arthropods such as mites, booklice, and springtails

The pincers (pedipalps) that look so big and imposing here are actually only a few millimeters long! But they do store venom that can be used to subdue small prey, such as mites, lice, and larvae.

WHAT IS IT?

House pseudoscorpions have eight legs and a small, rounded body that is easily mistaken for that of a tick. But they're not ticks either! These small arachnids usually live under tree bark or stones, or on the ground, though they're hard to spot. Other pseudoscorpion species may make their homes in caves, bird nests, or wasp nests. House pseudoscorpions are found in many parts of North America, as well as in Europe, Africa, and Australia.

Despite their name, house pseudoscorpions usually live among leaf litter, only sometimes coming into buildings.

HELPFUL, NOT HARMFUL!

Even when pseudoscorpions come into our homes, they cause no harm. They are too small to sting or bite humans, and they don't munch through wood like termites and some beetle larvae do. In fact, house pseudoscorpions can be helpful! They feed on small insects, mites, and other pests. Scientists have recently analyzed the venom that pseudoscorpions use on their prey and found that it contains chemicals that kill some disease-causing bacteria. This discovery might pave the way for new life-saving drugs in the future.

These tiny creatures are also known as book pseudoscorpions because they eat dust mites and lice found among dusty, old books.

COMMON EASTERN FIREFLY

There are few insects that seem more magical than fireflies. They're often known as "lightning bugs," but while lightning is bright, violent, and gone in an instant, these little beetles fly slowly through the dusk, their abdomens blinking on and off with a soft yellow light. Many creatures that live in the dark depths of the ocean produce light, but it is much rarer among animals on land. Fireflies really are special!

FACT FILE

- **Scientific name:** *Photinus pyralis*
- **Class:** insect
- **Length:** up to 0.5 in (1.4 cm)
- **Home:** moist places in meadows and woodlands, often near streams
- **Diet:** other insects, earthworms, and snails

Fireflies are most active at night, flashing their lights to communicate and find a mate. Although there are many different species, the common eastern firefly (*Photinus pyralis*) is one of the best known.

MAKING LIGHT

Fireflies glow during every stage of their life cycle—even their eggs glow! As adults, they have a special organ on their abdomen that makes light. Inside this organ, two chemicals called luciferase and luciferin combine with oxygen to make a gentle glow. Fireflies can turn their light on and off, creating short flashes. Their body controls the amount of oxygen that reaches the light organ—when there is enough oxygen, light is produced, but when the oxygen is restricted, there is no glow.

The process by which a firefly produces light, using a chemical reaction in its body, is called bioluminescence.

LARVAE LIFE

Firefly eggs hatch into flightless larvae that glow when it is dark. This glow warns predators that the larvae contain chemicals that taste bad and may even be deadly. Firefly larvae live for one to two years, burrowing into the soil during the winter to keep warm and emerging again in spring to feed. Eventually the larvae move back into the soil to complete the metamorphosis and take on their winged adult form. Adult fireflies only live for about a month, which they spend finding a mate.

Firefly larvae hunt on the ground for small insects, worms, and snails. They inject their prey with poison to paralyze it as they feed.

TRICKING A MATE

Male fireflies fly around, flashing their light to look for a partner. The females stay on the ground, looking for a flash. When they see the right kind of flash, they flash back. The male and female flash back and forth until they find each other and mate. However, the females of some different firefly species imitate the flash pattern of the common eastern firefly. They do this to trick the males and lure them in. But instead of mating, the females eat them!

This firefly (*Photuris lucicrescens*) looks harmless, but she can imitate the flashes of *Photinus pyralis* to secure a tasty meal!

***Photuris pensylvanica* lives in tidal areas along the east coast. It is threatened by habitat loss, rising seas, and light pollution.**

DISAPPEARING FIREFLIES

Fireflies were once a common sight in backyards and gardens during the summer twilight, but in recent decades there have been fewer and fewer of them. The common eastern firefly is not currently at risk of extinction, but many closely related species are. Fireflies are at risk because of habitat destruction, as wild landscapes are turned into roads and buildings. Light pollution is also a factor. Electric lights make it harder for fireflies to see each other's flashes and find a mate.

BLACK WIDOW

Thanks to a fierce-sounding name that could belong in a superhero film, the black widow spider is famous for being deadly. And it's true that these spiders are predators that can deliver a venomous bite to humans. But they are not huge, hairy-legged monsters. In fact, they're most dangerous to members of their own species. Black widow spiders are cannibals!

FACT FILE

- **Scientific name:** *Latrodectus mactans*
- **Class:** arachnid
- **Length:** females up to 0.4 in (10 mm) (not including the legs); males up to 0.1 in (4 mm)
- **Home:** dark sheltered spots in many different parts of North America
- **Diet:** insects and other arthropods

LOVE AND DEATH

Black widow spiders get their name because of the belief that the females eat the males once mating has finished. This does sometimes happen, but it's fairly rare—though there are other closely related species in South America where it is more common. After mating, the female lays several hundred eggs in a sac that she spins. Once they hatch, the bigger juveniles often eat the smaller ones. Perhaps they're the deadliest black widows of all!

This female black widow is guarding an egg sac. The male is smaller and brownish-gray, with spots rather than an hourglass marking.

Female black widow spiders are shiny and black, with a distinctive red hourglass shape on their abdomen.

HELPING AND HARMING

Black widow venom is toxic to humans, but these small spiders are not aggressive and will only bite if threatened. The bite can be painful and is usually not serious, except in rare cases. In fact, black widow spiders probably help us more than they harm us. They eat disease-carrying flies and mosquitoes, as well as other insects that damage crops. Scientists are also studying their venom to see if it can be used to make more natural insecticides.

Black widows will often catch and eat prey that is larger than themselves, such as this grasshopper that's become entangled in the spider's silk.

GIANT MAYFLY

If you like to fish, you'll probably already be familiar with mayflies. These insects are a favorite meal of many fish species, so they're often used as bait. People even make artificial versions of mayflies as fishing lures. There are mayflies all over the world, and the giant mayfly is one of the largest species found in North America.

FACT FILE

- **Scientific name:** *Hexagenia limbata*
- **Class:** insect
- **Length:** body up to 1.1 in (2.7 cm)
- **Home:** nymphs live in lakes and streams across North America; adults fly near the shores
- **Diet:** nymphs eat algae and organic matter; adults do not feed

GROWING STAGES

Young mayfly nymphs are wingless and live along the bottoms of lakes and streams. They have gills to take in oxygen from the water. Some species burrow into the sediment there and feed on tiny specks of organic matter that fall into their burrow. Others scrape algae from rocks. As a nymph grows, it can go through as many as 30 molts. Then it swims to the surface and molts again to become a subimago, with wings. After a day or two, one final molt turns the subimago into an imago (adult) mayfly.

All mayfly nymphs look similar to adults, but they have three tail filaments instead of two, and they have mandibles for burrowing and eating. This nymph is scraping algae from a rock.

HERE TODAY, GONE TOMORROW

Mayflies get their name because in many species, the adults emerge in May. These insects belong to an insect order called Ephemeroptera. The *ptera* part of the name means "wing," but in ancient Greek, *ephemeros* meant "lasting only one day." This is because adult mayflies live for only a day or two. They have no functional mouthparts, so they cannot eat. They devote what energy they have to finding a mate and laying eggs.

Adult mayflies tend to emerge all at once, creating large swarms of insects frantically trying to mate during their short life, before it's too late.

An adult mayfly has two long tails called cerci at the end of its abdomen. They help it to keep stable when flying.

PERIODICAL CICADA

In the eastern parts of Canada and the United States, summer evenings are often accompanied by a buzzing sound that gently rises and falls. This is the noise made by large numbers of cicadas. There are cicadas all over the world, but periodical cicadas live only in North America. Unlike other species, which are active every year, periodical cicadas have a much longer life cycle.

FACT FILE

- **Scientific name:** *Magicicada septendecim*
- **Class:** insect
- **Length:** up to 1.6 in (4 cm)
- **Home:** nymphs live in soil amongst deciduous trees
- **Diet:** nymphs feed on plant root juices; adults feed on plant sap

WAITING GAME

A female periodical cicada lays her eggs in the twigs of a tree. When they hatch, the nymphs make their way to the ground and burrow their way into the soil. There they feed on juices from plant roots. The nymphs stay underground for 17 years, going through four molts during that time, moving deeper underground with each molt. When the 17 years are up, they build tunnels to the surface in the spring, waiting for the right moment to emerge, when the soil temperature reaches about 64 °F (18 °C).

This cicada nymph is emerging from the ground after 17 years. It will go through one final molt to reach its adult form.

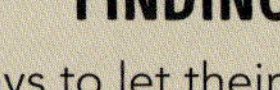

FINDING A MATE

After resting for a few days to let their new exoskeletons harden completely, male cicadas begin "singing" loudly to attract a mate. They have structures called tymbals on their abdomen. Vibrating their abdominal muscles makes the tymbals move and creates a sound, and they often do this in large groups called choruses. Adult cicadas have only a few weeks left to live, so they must make the most of their time. Once they have mated, the female deposits batches of eggs in the trees—usually several hundred eggs in total. Once she has laid her eggs, she dies.

This male cicada has raised its wing, revealing a sound-making organ—or tymbal—on the side of its first abdominal segment. When this organ moves, it creates a sound used as a mating song.

Adult periodical cicadas have browny-black bodies and red eyes. The adults live for just a few weeks, although they've lived underground as nymphs for over a decade.

WHY WAIT?

There are thousands of cicada species around the world, but only a handful have a long life cycle. Scientists have several theories about why some have developed this strategy. One idea is it allows the cicadas to outlive their main predators, such as birds and squirrels. New generations of predators can't predict when cicadas will emerge. Likewise, creatures with shorter lifespans can't specialize in living on periodical cicadas, since the cicadas are not around often enough.

Although this bullfrog has successfully captured a cicada to eat, there are plenty more cicadas that will live long enough to mate and lay eggs.

CICADAS EVERYWHERE!

There are several closely related species of periodical cicada living in eastern North America. Some have a 13-year life cycle and others have a 17-year cycle. Every five or six years, a 13-year brood and a 17-year brood will emerge in the same year, though not necessarily in the same part of the continent. In 2024, two huge broods emerged close together. In the states of Illinois and Missouri, the sound of the mating song of trillions of cicadas was said to be "deafening."

When the periodical cicadas molt into their adult form, they leave their empty shells behind, often littering the landscape.

EASTERN TENT CATERPILLAR

Many caterpillars live solitary lives, but other species are known as social caterpillars. A group of siblings hatches out together and then stays together as they forage for food. The eastern tent caterpillar is a moth species with some of the most social caterpillars of all. Before they become moths, the caterpillars live together in a silken "tent" that they create. There is safety in numbers, and the caterpillars are able to warn each other of any dangers.

FACT FILE

- **Scientific name:** *Malacosoma americanum*
- **Class:** insect
- **Length:** caterpillars up to 2 in (5 cm); adult moths up to 1 in (2.5 cm) wingspan
- **Home:** forested areas of the eastern and central United States
- **Diet:** caterpillars eat leaves; adults do not feed

KEEPING SAFE

A group of tent caterpillars is called a cohort, and it can have up to 200 individuals. The caterpillars can produce thin, strong silk from a spinneret, rather like a spider does—but this tubelike structure is found on the lower side of the caterpillar's mouth. They work together to build a tent in the space where tree branches meet the trunk. When not feeding, they stay together in this tent, which provides protection from parasites and some predators.

The eastern tent caterpillar has irritating bristles to deter predators. When threatened, it can also rear up and thrash its body.

TIMING IT RIGHT

Eastern tent caterpillars hatch from eggs laid in late spring or early summer on a tree branch. Inside the egg, the caterpillars are in a kind of suspended animation. They will not hatch until the next spring, when there will be plenty of leaves to eat. Once they hatch, they eat, grow, and molt five times—a process that takes about six weeks. Then they go off alone to spin a silk cocoon where their bodies change into adult moths. The moths have less than a week to find a mate and lay eggs before they die.

Male eastern tent caterpillar moths have feathery antennae to help them detect the scent of a female, for mating.

Fruit trees, such as peach, cherry, or apple, form an ideal structure on which to base the caterpillars' tent. As the caterpillars grow, they work to make the tent bigger, too.

WESTERN YELLOWJACKET

No one wants wasps at their picnic, and there's a good reason for that! They can be annoying, trying to feed on anything sugary, and if they feel threatened they can sting. Unlike honeybees, which can sting only once, wasps like yellowjackets can sting a victim over and over. These wasps may feel like a nuisance, but they're important—they help farmers by destroying insects that attack crops.

FACT FILE

- **Scientific name:** *Vespula pensylvanica*
- **Class:** insect
- **Length:** up to 0.6 in (1.5 cm)
- **Home:** can live in many different habitats in western North America
- **Diet:** larvae eat other arthropods; adult wasps feed on nectar and fruit juices

QUEENS AND WORKERS

Western yellowjackets live in colonies, similar to bees. Each colony has a queen, who is in charge. She builds the first nest and lays eggs in the spring. These eggs will all hatch into female workers. Once these workers are adults, they will help enlarge the nest and find food. When the queen lays more eggs in late summer, the female workers will also look after them. These eggs hatch into male wasps and new queens, who will go on to mate and start a new colony. Only the queens survive by hibernating during the winter.

These yellowjacket workers are flying to and from the nest to bring food for their queen.

Yellowjackets feed on sugary substances, such as the nectar on this fennel plant.

IN THE NEST

The nest of a western yellowjacket colony is made from chewed-up plant fibers, and it has many small hexagonal cells. The queen lays one egg in each cell. Once they hatch, the larvae remain in their cells as they develop. When they're hungry, they wriggle. That signal tells the worker wasps to go and find prey. Then they bring it back and chew it up, to feed the paste to the larvae. Soon the larvae will pupate and turn into adult wasps.

In a wasp's nest, each larva grows and molts in its own hexagonal cell. Then it spins a silken cap over the cell, to pupate into an adult wasp.

GOLDEN TORTOISE BEETLE

Gardeners in North America who find the leaves of their morning glory plants dotted with holes know that it's likely the work of the golden tortoise beetle. This small but stunning insect, which looks like a tiny golden brooch, lives in many parts of the continent. It feeds on the leaves of plants in one particular family, which includes morning glory as well as sweet potato and bindweed.

FACT FILE

- **Scientific name:** *Charidotella sexpunctata*
- **Class:** insect
- **Length:** up to 0.3 in (7 mm)
- **Home:** plants such as sweet potato
- **Diet:** leaves

When golden tortoise beetles chew holes in leaves, it doesn't kill the plants, but can make them look unattractive.

SAFE UNDER A SHELL

The golden tortoise beetle's glossy body is covered by a transparent oval shield, a bit like a tortoise's shell. If the beetle feels threatened, it can pull its legs and antennae under the shell to keep safe, just like a tortoise does. The larvae of this species also make use of a shield, but theirs is much more gross. A larva squirts a mixture of its own poop and parts of its old exoskeleton onto its back, where it hardens to form a shield, as shown below. This protects the larva's soft body from predators, and looks pretty stinky, which probably deters them as well!

A golden tortoise beetle larva can lift and lower the protective "poop shield" with its rear spines if it needs to.

CHANGING COLOR

Golden tortoise beetles usually look shiny and metallic, but they can sometimes appear orangey-red with black spots instead, as in the image below. This is because their gold color is created by a thin layer of liquid inside their body, which hides their true color. When a beetle is scared, the liquid layer thins out and the gold color disappears, revealing the orangey-red underneath to warn off predators. When the beetle feels safe, the liquid thickens and it becomes gold again.

The *sexpunctata* of the beetle's species name means "six-spotted," but you can only see the black spots when it feels threatened, or during mating.

CANDY-STRIPED LEAFHOPPER

With their bright red and green or blue markings giving them the appearance of a holiday candy, these tiny bugs look good enough to eat! Leafhoppers use their wings and strong hind legs to fly and leap from plant to plant, looking for food and to escape predators. The nymphs are born wingless, with a pale white or cream color. As they molt and get bigger, they gradually develop wings and colored markings.

FACT FILE

- **Scientific name:** *Graphocephala coccinea*
- **Class:** insect
- **Length:** up to 0.3 in (8 mm)
- **Home:** wooded areas in eastern North America, particularly near the coast
- **Diet:** plant sap

Leafhoppers often eat more than they need to. They eject extra sap from their abdomen. We call this sugary, sticky liquid "honeydew."

SAP SUCKERS

Candy-striped leafhoppers feed on plant sap, using their special mouthparts to pierce the leaves and stems before sucking out the sugary goodness. They often choose fruit bushes, such as blackberry or raspberry, as well as rhododendrons, roses, and grape vines. Adult leafhoppers lay their eggs inside the plant stems or leaves. When the nymphs emerge in the spring, there are plenty of fresh new leaves for them to eat.

Candy-striped leafhoppers can jump 40 times their body length, to look for food or escape danger, thanks to long and powerful hind legs.

PLANT PESTS

Candy-striped leafhoppers may look cool, but you definitely don't want them in your garden. Their habit of feeding on sap and injecting eggs into plants can damage the host plants. They can also pass on a bacterium in their saliva, which makes parts of the leaves turn brown and dry. Leafhoppers are such fast movers that they're difficult to catch, but spiders, lacewings, and ladybugs like to eat them. These predators help to keep leafhopper populations under control.

The bacterium in the leafhopper's saliva has caused Pierce's disease in this American elm tree, resulting in scorched-looking leaves.

MONARCH BUTTERFLY

Every year in North America, an incredible migration takes place. Millions of orange and black monarch butterflies fly thousands of kilometres to find a warm place to spend the winter. The butterflies always go to the same places in the winter, but the amazing thing is that no butterfly makes the journey twice. They can't learn it from their parents. Their genes tell them what to do!

FACT FILE

- **Scientific name:** *Danaus plexippus*
- **Class:** insect
- **Length:** caterpillars up to 1.7 in (4.5 cm); adults' wingspan up to 4.8 in (12.4 cm)
- **Home:** anywhere in North America where milkweeds grow
- **Diet:** caterpillars eat milkweed plants; adults feed on nectar from flowers

Adult monarch butterflies often feed on daisies. These are a good source of nectar, which is easy to reach in the flowers' open heads.

This monarch caterpillar has grown about ten times its size since it hatched. It eats so much that it grows very quickly.

FROM CATERPILLAR TO BUTTERFLY

Monarch butterflies lay their eggs on the leaves of the milkweed plant. When the caterpillars hatch, they eat the egg casing and then get to work on the leaves. After its first molt, the caterpillar has black, white, and yellow stripes. It goes through three more molts and then, when it is about two weeks old, it forms a chrysalis. The chrysalis is pale green to keep it camouflaged against the leaves. Inside the chrysalis, the caterpillar changes into a butterfly (see page 12).

WARNING: DANGER!

The milkweed plants that monarchs eat contain chemicals that are toxic to most animal species. But the chemicals don't hurt the monarchs, even when they build up in their bodies. The bright colors of monarch caterpillars and butterflies act as a warning to predators, telling them that they're poisonous. Other species that aren't poisonous have evolved to copy the monarch's appearance, so they don't get eaten either.

This viceroy butterfly is not poisonous, but many predators can't tell it apart from a monarch.

Migrating monarchs never return home but they produce the next generation of butterflies—one will soon emerge from this chrysalis.

ON THE MOVE

Monarch butterflies that emerge in late summer or early fall don't look for mates or lay eggs. Instead, they prepare for a long journey south. As they fly, they keep fueled up on nectar. Once they reach their warm winter home, they roost in trees through the winter. In spring, they mate and begin a journey north, looking for milkweed plants to lay their eggs. These eggs hatch into caterpillars that will eventually finish the journey back to their parents' original home. Monarch butterflies are sensitive to changing temperatures, so climate change can disrupt their migratory patterns and life cycle.

EAST AND WEST

Monarchs in North America fall into one of two groups. Those that live west of the Rocky Mountains migrate to the Californian coast during the winter. There, they roost in eucalyptus, pine, or cypress trees. Monarchs that live east of the Rockies travel to the mountains of central Mexico. Forests of oyamel fir trees are found high on the mountain slopes, and it is here that the monarchs roost, staying still to avoid using too much energy.

Monarchs cluster together and cling to the needles of oyamel trees, which help to protect them from mountain wind and snow.

IO MOTH

The stunning io moth is often seen on summer nights in the eastern half of North America. The female releases a special chemical signal to attract a male. They then mate, and the female lays eggs on the leaves of trees. The leaves provide food for the caterpillars once they hatch. Io moth caterpillars are covered in venomous spines, which deliver a nasty sting to predators—or any human unlucky enough to touch one.

FACT FILE

- **Scientific name:** *Automeris io*
- **Class:** insect
- **Length:** caterpillars up to 2.7 in (7 cm); adults' wingspan up to 3.5 in (9 cm)
- **Home:** woodlands and meadows from southern Canada to Central America
- **Diet:** caterpillars eat leaves; adults do not feed

The yellow color of a male io moth really stands out. This is a warning to predators to stay away.

MOVING AROUND

Io moths lay their eggs in clusters, and when the caterpillars hatch out, they tend to stay together. They travel in groups of up to 40 caterpillars, following each other's silk trail, but as they grow older they begin to travel alone. The first few instars of an io moth caterpillar are reddish-brown, but by the fifth instar they have a feathery, green appearance. Like most caterpillars, they have six legs as well as five pairs of prolegs, which offer a good grip.

A caterpillar's prolegs are stumplike appendages that act a bit like spiky suction cups or hooks, to help them navigate tricky leaves, vines, or branches.

LOOK AT ME!

Io moths have a pair of large dark spots on their hindwings that look like eyes, and many other butterfly and moth species do too. These spots aren't camouflage—in fact, they make the moths stand out! If an io moth suddenly uncovers its eyespots, it might trick a predator into thinking that they're about to attack a larger and more dangerous animal, such as an owl. The eyespots might also be a distraction, leading predators to attack the moth's wings rather than its body and vital organs.

Unlike the bright yellow males, females have brown forewings. But they too have large eyespots on their hindwings.

WHEEL BUG

This insect is part of a group known as assassin bugs, and for good reason—it's a fierce predator from the moment it hatches out of its egg. The species known as the wheel bug gets its name because of the odd, spiky structure on its back. It looks a lot like a saw wheel, or a gear with teeth around the rim.

FACT FILE

- **Scientific name:** *Arilus cristatus*
- **Class:** insect
- **Length:** adults up to 1.2 in (3 cm)
- **Home:** leafy areas of the United States and Central America
- **Diet:** other arthropods

As well as their distinctive back, wheel bugs have a curved beak. This contains mouthparts used to pierce its prey and suck up juices.

HUNTING FOR FOOD

Wheel bugs prey on whatever they can catch. They use their mouthparts to inject a type of venom that kills the prey and breaks it down from the inside, so they can suck out the liquefied interior. Gardeners don't mind wheel bugs because they kill pests, such as beetles and caterpillars, which eat their plants. However, they must treat these bugs with care—both nymphs and adults can deliver a very painful bite if they feel threatened.

Wheel bugs use their front legs to grip and pin their prey, such as this bee, before injecting it with venom.

WHAT'S WITH THE WHEEL?

There are many other species of assassin bug, but none of them have a toothed wheel on their back like wheel bugs do. So what's it for? Unfortunately, no one knows for certain! It might help them recognize other members of the same species, or warn predators that they are dangerous. Perhaps the spiky nubs on the wheel make wheel bugs unpleasant to eat.

Before they reach their adult phase, wheel bug nymphs are red and black, with no wheel shape on their back.

HARVESTMAN

Anyone with a fear of spiders might easily be creeped out by a harvestman. With their round bodies and long, spindly legs, these creatures certainly look like spiders. But they're not! Harvestmen—more commonly known as daddy longlegs in North America—are arachnids, like spiders, but they form a different group. There are species found all over the world. This species originated in Eurasia and has been introduced to North America.

FACT FILE

- **Scientific name:** *Phalangium opilio*
- **Class:** arachnid
- **Length:** body up to 0.4 in (9 mm)
- **Home:** non-desert areas of Canada and the United States
- **Diet:** soft-bodied animals such as aphids, caterpillars, and beetle larvae

STAYING SAFE

These harvestmen come out at night to look for food or find a mate. Their dull brown colors help them to blend in with dead leaves and make them harder for predators to spot. If threatened, they sometimes release a bad-smelling liquid or vibrate their bodies rapidly so they're harder to grab hold of. If a predator does manage to seize a leg, the harvestman can detach it. The leg will continue to twitch, distracting the predator while the harvestman makes a quick escape.

Like all arachnids, harvestmen have appendages (see page 9), which they use to hold, cut, or crush their prey. These are longer in the male, shown here.

NOT A SPIDER!

Harvestmen and spiders both have eight legs, but the similarities stop there. These two arachnids are not closely related, and if you look carefully, you'll find plenty of differences. A spider's body is divided into two parts, while a harvestman has only one. Spiders have more eyes, and have glands for producing silk and venom. Harvestmen don't make silk or spin webs, and they don't have a venomous bite either. They're pretty harmless!

Most harvestmen have two eyes, like this spring harvestman (*Rilaena triangularis*). Some species adapted to living in dark caves have none at all.

The harvestman's long, thin legs help it to span large distances between leaves and twigs as it clambers across vegetation.

GREEN LACEWING

There's no prize for guessing how the lacewing got its name! These insects have delicate, transparent wings with darker veins running through them that look like the cloth known as lace. There are species of lacewing found all over the world. Many species of green lacewing, with beautiful green bodies, live in North America.

FACT FILE

- **Scientific name:** *Chrysoperla rufilabris*
- **Class:** insect
- **Length:** larvae up to 0.6 in (1.5 cm); adults up to 0.8 in (2 cm)
- **Home:** leafy areas in eastern North America
- **Diet:** larvae eat soft-bodied insects; adults eat pollen and honeydew (see page 31)

DEADLY LARVAE

While adult lacewings look beautiful and dainty, their larvae are completely different. They have a squat, crocodile-shaped body and are often known as "aphid lions." They are fierce predators who hunt and kill soft-bodied arthropods, such as aphids. A single larva can eat around 200 aphids in a week. This is helpful to farmers, as aphids are a pest that damage crops. The larvae also eat the eggs and larvae of other insect pests.

Lacewing larvae have spiky hairs on their body to deter predators. The spikes also collect debris which helps them to stay more camouflaged.

PRECIOUS EGGS

Once they hatch, lacewing larvae feed and grow for up to three weeks. Then they construct an oval cocoon, where they will spend about 10 days as their body changes. Adults emerge and feed on pollen and sweet sap and live for up to six weeks, depending on the climate. After mating, the female lays her eggs—each one at the tip of a separate stalk made from silk.

Keeping the eggs separate like this helps to prevent the larvae from eating each other once they hatch.

Adult green lacewings are particularly active in the evening or at night. Their delicate wings are longer than their body, giving them a relatively slow, fluttering flight.

SOUTH AMERICA

South America is a land of great diversity, stretching from tropical regions north of the Equator to areas of cold, barren tundra at the southern tip. The continent is home to the Amazon, the world's largest tropical rainforest, as well as wetlands, grasslands, and high mountain peaks. The Amazon is known for its huge range of wildlife, but there are bugs living in all parts of South America.

The high Andes Mountains are cold and windy, but flies and mosquitoes have adapted to survive here.

Dense plant life in the Amazon rainforest provides food and shelter for many bugs, such as ants, butterflies, and beetles.

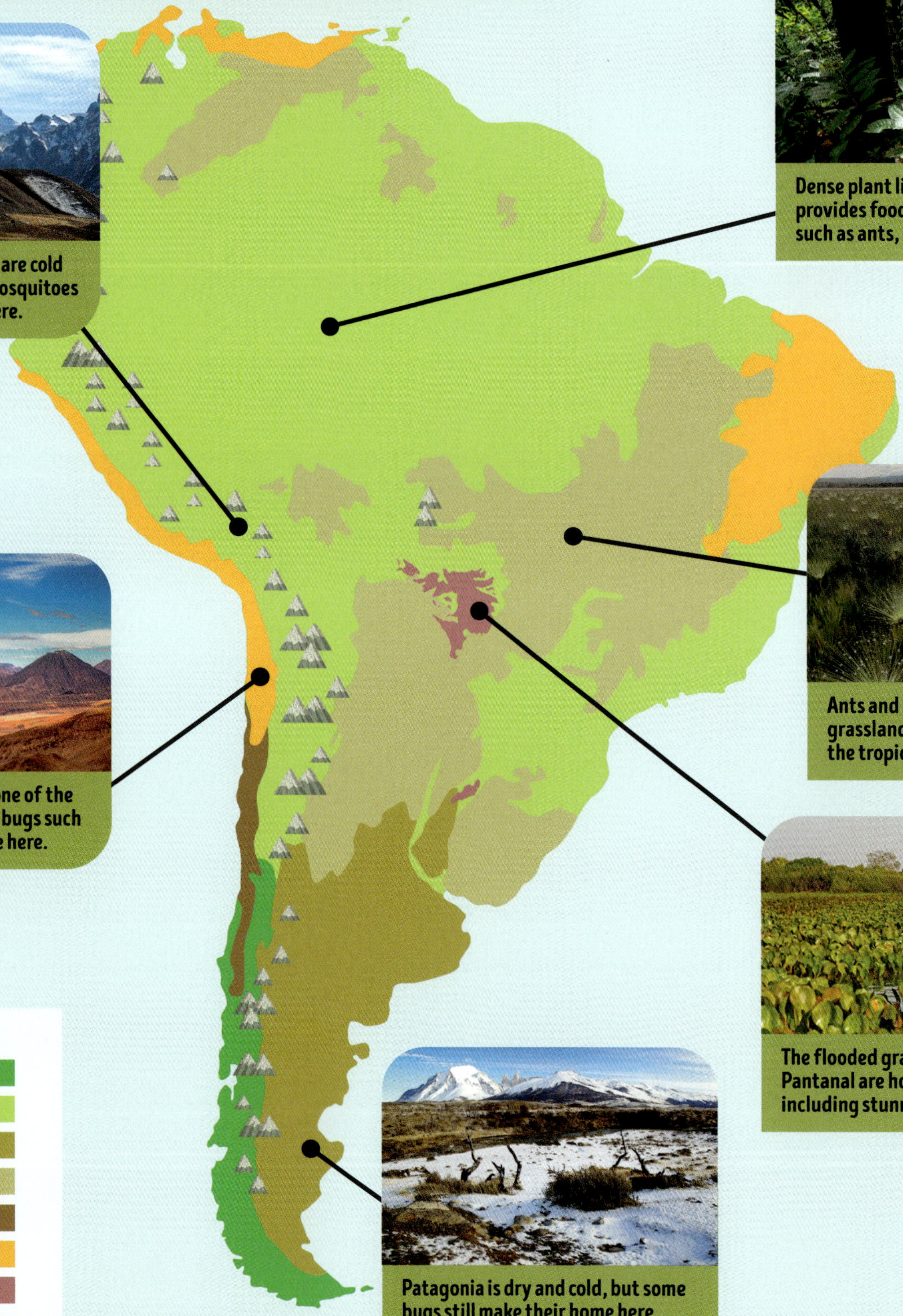

Chile's Atacama Desert is one of the driest places on Earth, but bugs such as wasps and scorpions live here.

Ants and moths thrive in the large grasslands of South America, such as the tropical Cerrado in the center.

The flooded grasslands of the Pantanal are home to many insects, including stunning butterflies.

MAP KEY

- Temperate Forest
- Tropical Forest
- Temperate Grassland
- Tropical Grassland
- Shrubland
- Desert
- Wetlands
- Mountains

Patagonia is dry and cold, but some bugs still make their home here, such as mayflies and mosquitoes.

TITAN BEETLE

It comes as no surprise that the huge Amazon rainforest is also home to one of the world's largest insects! The titan beetle is a true whopper. You'd think that scientists would have discovered everything there is to know about a record-breaker like this, but the titan beetle's life is still a bit of a mystery.

FACT FILE

- **Scientific name:** *Titanus giganteus*
- **Class:** insect
- **Length:** larvae unknown; adults up to 6.5 in (16.5 cm)
- **Home:** tropical rainforests
- **Diet:** wood and other plants

The titan beetle grows nearly as long as a man's hand, with powerful mandibles strong enough to bite through a pencil.

WHAT WE KNOW

Titan beetles belong to a group called longhorn beetles. Only the Hercules beetle (see page 48) is longer, but much of its length is made up of a giant horn. When it comes to body length and weight, the titan beetle has it beat. In fact, titan beetles are too heavy to take off from the ground. Females can't fly at all, but if a male wants to take flight it must climb a tree and launch itself from there.

The male titan beetle's hindwings, as seen in this artwork, are short compared to other longhorn beetles. The females have no hindwings at all.

LOTS TO LEARN

There is a lot that we don't know about this insect. In fact, no one has ever found a titan beetle larva! Based on the size of the adult beetles, they must be huge. We think the larvae bore into trees, where they feed on wood and grow in secret. We don't know how many times they molt, or how the adults mate or how long they live. Hopefully the entomologists of the future will find the answers to these questions!

We know that titan beetles have large compound eyes that take up about a third of their head, suggesting they have a wide field of vision.

THORN BUG

Thorn bugs are a type of treehopper—a large group of insects that live in trees and have powerful hind legs for jumping. Treehoppers come in many unusual shapes, and it's clear to see how the sharp-bodied thorn bug got its name! This unusual body structure allows thorn bugs to hide in plain sight on the stalks of the plants where they live.

FACT FILE

- **Scientific name:** genus *Umbonia* (several species)
- **Class:** insect
- **Length:** up to 0.4 in (10 mm)
- **Home:** tropical forests
- **Diet:** plant sap

PLANT LIFE

Female thorn bugs lay their eggs on a host plant. When the eggs hatch, the nymphs use their sharp mouthparts to pierce the plant and suck out its sweet sap. The nymphs look similar to adults, but with no wings, and they will molt five times. Each instar is bigger than the last, with more developed wings. Adult male thorn bugs can fly to find mates. Thorn bugs also leap from plant to plant, often turning somersaults in midair!

This twig looks like it's covered in thorns, but it's actually a dense cluster of thorn bugs.

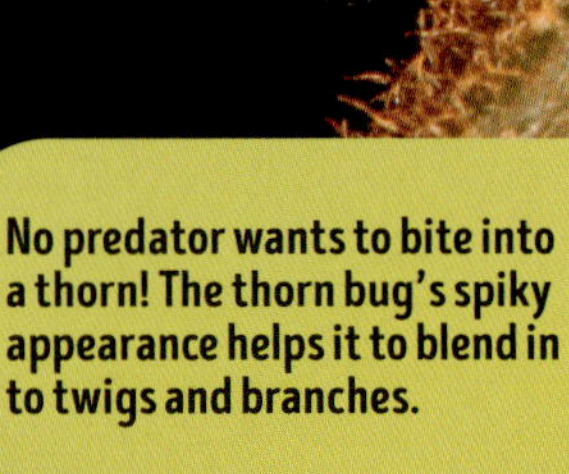

No predator wants to bite into a thorn! The thorn bug's spiky appearance helps it to blend in to twigs and branches.

A THORNY QUESTION

A thorn bug's "thorn" is part of its thorax. An insect's thorax is divided into three segments, each with a pair of legs. Any wings are attached to the second and third sections. The first section—called the "prothorax"—never has wings, and in treehoppers it has evolved into a range of weird shapes. These shapes provide camouflage or help the treehopper to look like something else. Many look like thorns, while others look like twigs, leaves, or even ants!

Other species of treehopper have equally unusual body shapes—check these ones out!

GLASSWING BUTTERFLY

Butterfly wings come in a range of stunning, vibrant colors, but only a few have wings that are see-through! The delicate wings of the glasswing butterfly look like tiny stained-glass windows, with black veins separating "panes" that are completely transparent. These clear wings help the butterflies to hide from predators, such as birds.

FACT FILE

- **Scientific name:** *Greta oto*
- **Class:** insect
- **Length:** caterpillars up to 1 in (2.5 cm); adults' wingspan up to 2.4 in (6 cm)
- **Home:** tropical rainforests in Central and South America
- **Diet:** caterpillars eat leaves; adults feed on nectar

Like other butterflies, the glasswing butterfly curls up its proboscis when it's not feeding. When it's time to eat, it will use this straw-like tube to suck up nectar.

TOXIC TOTS

Glasswing butterflies usually lay their eggs on plants in the genus *Cestrum*, also known as jessamine. These plants are part of the same family as deadly nightshade, and they contain toxins that are poisonous to many animals. But the caterpillars aren't harmed by eating them, and they store up the chemicals, making their own bodies poisonous to predators. Adults feed on the nectar of a different kind of poisonous plant, making their bodies toxic as well.

Glasswing butterfly caterpillars are well camouflaged as well as poisonous.

DECEPTIVE APPEARANCE

Glasswing butterflies look fragile and delicate, but they're actually surprisingly tough. They are fast fliers that regularly migrate to different locations, traveling up to 12 miles (19 km) per day. Males come together in large groups to show off and compete for mates by defending small territories. This process is called "lekking." As they fly, the males also release chemicals that females find attractive.

The chrysalis of this glasswing butterfly is firmly attached to a leaf, keeping it safely in place as the butterfly emerges.

FIRE ANT

Named after their reddish-brown color as well as their searing sting, fire ants can really pack a punch. These tiny creatures are full of team spirit, working together and watching each other's back. When they feel threatened, the pheromones they release cause the ants to swarm and sting *en masse*, overpowering small creatures, such as lizards and birds. Originating in South America, fire ants can now be found on almost every continent.

FACT FILE

- **Scientific name:** *Solenopsis invicta*
- **Class:** insect
- **Length:** up to 0.2 in (5 mm)
- **Home:** underground tunnels, mounds, or nests in trees
- **Diet:** small insects, seeds and seedlings

WELL TRAVELED

Fire ants are now found far beyond their original South American habitats. They were first detected in North America in the 1930s, having been carried there in contaminated soil used as ballast (stabilizer) in merchant ships. The shipping of contaminated goods, such as plants, has also seen them spread further afield to Asia, Africa, Oceania, and now parts of Europe. The ants nest in soil, rotting wood, and the cavities of plants, and sometimes make their way into buildings.

Fire ants are seen here swarming over a boot. When you come across a group of fire ants, they could belong to a colony of up to 250,000 individuals!

WATER BABIES

Fire ants evolved in the subtropical Pantanal wetlands of South America (see page 38). In flood conditions, their unique survival instinct kicks in. The ants carry unhatched eggs from their nest and, as the water starts to rise, the ants' legs link together, forming a life raft. The ants can stay afloat like this, without food, for almost two weeks, helping them to reach new, safer nesting grounds. Some rafts have been known to exceed 100,000 ants.

These fire ants made a raft when rain submerged their nesting ground. The ants' bodies form the raft, which is anchored to blades of grass.

These fire ants are navigating a tree branch as they forage for food. Their strong mandibles are used to harvest seeds and capture small prey, as well as for lifting and carrying their young.

FRIEND OR FOE?

In urban areas, fire ants have been known to keep nuisance pests in check—such as fleas, ticks, and chiggers—but fire ants can also cause structural damage if they build their nests under concrete or chew through electrical equipment. The ants can be particularly threatening to farmland, eating seeds and damaging shoots. Fire ant stings cause a burning sensation, which gives the insect its name. The stings are usually harmless to humans, but can cause a severe allergic reaction in rare cases. Globally, up to $32 billion is spent each year to deal with fire ants.

At the end of a fire ant's mandibles are four tiny teeth. The mandibles are strong enough to cut through electrical cables and telephone wires.

KEEPING CONTROL

Insecticides have been used to control the spread of fire ants, but more natural methods include quarantining imported products and using viruses or encouraging parasites. Scientists have found, for example, that an electric current stimulates fire ants to release a scent that attracts parasitic phorid flies. These are like nature's flying guillotine. Female phorid flies inject their eggs into the bodies of fire ants, and the resulting larva moves into the ant's head where it feeds and grows. The larva releases a membrane-dissolving enzyme that causes the ant's head to fall off!

Here, a gray phorid fly is seen emerging from the red head of a decapitated fire ant, which has served as its host.

GIANT FLY

Flies can be a nuisance as they buzz around, landing on food and getting in the way. But most of the flies that come into our homes are a very minor annoyance compared to this giant fly that lives in Brazil and other parts of South America. It's a true whopper, with a body as big as your finger and a wingspan to match. In fact, it's the largest species of fly ever found!

FACT FILE

- **Scientific name:** *Gauromydas heros*
- **Class:** insect
- **Length:** up to 2.8 in (7 cm); wingspan up to 4 in (10 cm)
- **Home:** wooded areas in South America
- **Diet:** larvae eat other insect larvae; adults probably feed on nectar

MYSTERY FLY

This species might be big, but it's also rare and secretive. It tends to live in the wilderness rather than buzzing around buildings, and the adults live only for a few days or weeks. However, we do know that the females lay their eggs in or near leafcutter ant nests, and the larvae feed on the larvae of various beetle species that scavenge on ant waste. With their short adult lifespan, finding a mate is key. Adult males often wait near ant nests, for a female pupa to emerge.

This artwork shows a giant fly pupa emerging from a soil chamber, before she molts into her adult form. A male giant fly is waiting nearby to mate with her.

TRULY THE BIGGEST?

For years, this species has held the crown as the world's largest known fly, but there's a chance it could be knocked off its perch in the future. Researchers have come across old specimens of two different fly species in the same genus, found in the 1930s in Argentina and Brazil. Neither specimen was a record-breaker, but the scientists believe other members of these two species might be even bigger—if only they could find more examples out there to prove it!

As this specimen shows, the giant fly is a record-breaker for size, but will it one day lose the top spot?

Sightings of this giant fly are rare, and many researchers have never even seen one in the wild!

HARLEQUIN BEETLE

The harlequin beetle gets its name because of the striking red, orange, brown, and black pattern on its back, which makes it look like the checkered costume of the harlequin, a character from medieval European plays. Usually, when an animal has bright colors or patterns on its body, it's a warning that it's poisonous. However, these beetles are not poisonous, and the pattern actually helps them to blend in on some lichen-covered tree trunks.

FACT FILE

- **Scientific name:** *Acrocinus longimanus*
- **Class:** insect
- **Length:** body up to 3 in (7.6 cm)
- **Home:** tropical forests
- **Diet:** larvae feed on wood and fungi; adults feed on tree sap

TREE LOVERS

Harlequin beetles love trees, particularly ones that have recently fallen. These provide the best place to lay their eggs, and female beetles can sniff them out by smelling the sap that the trees release when they fall. The beetle's long antennae are particularly good at sensing smells. The females lay their eggs under the bark, and the larvae eat the tree's wood and fungi once they hatch. Once they pupate, the adult beetles can live for several months, feeding on tree sap.

The harlequin beetle's long antennae can often be longer than the length of its body! These are used to sense their surroundings.

Male harlequin beetles have extremely long front legs, used to fight other males and to defend their territory. Females are a similar color but have shorter front legs.

HITCHHIKERS

Harlequin beetles have an unusual relationship with tiny arachnids called pseudoscorpions (see page 21), which often live beneath their wing cases. Unlike the harlequin beetle, pseudoscorpions cannot fly. So when they want to travel, they hitch a lift! When the beetle takes flight, the pseudoscorpions attach themselves to its abdomen with silk threads that they spin from their chelicerae (or jaws, see page 9). Once the beetle lands, the pseudoscorpions start a new colony in this new location.

This pseudoscorpion has hitched a lift on a harlequin beetle, securing itself with silk threads. This form of travel helps it to find new food sources or a potential mate.

AMAZONIAN GIANT CENTIPEDE

Most bugs are on the small side, but the Amazonian giant centipede really breaks the mold! Growing up to 12 inches (30 cm) long, this fierce predator lives in the tropical rainforests of South America. It's also fairly long-lived for a bug, surviving up to 10 years or more. That's a lot of time to spend terrorizing the other rainforest wildlife!

FACT FILE

- **Scientific name:** *Scolopendra gigantea*
- **Class:** myriapod
- **Length:** up to 12 in (30 cm)
- **Home:** damp tropical rainforests
- **Diet:** small animals

STRONG HUNTERS

Giant centipedes are fierce predators, big enough to take on prey such as lizards, mice, bats, and scorpions. They will eat whatever they can catch. As their eyesight is not very good, they rely on their antennae to find prey. These centipedes are fast runners, and they use their pincers to inject venom into their prey to paralyze it. They will attack humans if they feel threatened, and their venom is strong enough to be very painful.

Giant centipedes use their long, strong bodies to pin their prey, like this snake, while the venom gets to work.

Amazonian giant centipedes reach the size of a 12 inch (30 cm) ruler—and it's rare to see one exposed like this during the day.

KEEPING HYDRATED

Centipedes lose water through their exoskeleton, meaning it's easy for them to become dehydrated. To avoid this, they live in very moist environments. Amazonian giant centipedes spend the heat of the day hiding in leaf litter or under rocks, only coming out at night to feed. If they are spotted by a predator, they sprint away to a safe hiding place.

Centipedes are often preyed upon by large birds, such as owls, as well as spiders and small mammals.

GIANT OWL BUTTERFLY

Owl butterflies take their name from the eyespots on the underside of their hind wings, which look like the bright, inquisitive eyes of a hungry owl. They often live on banana plantations. There, the adult butterflies help farmers by pollinating the plants as they feed on nectar and fruit. However, their caterpillars are seen as pests, as they have huge appetites for the leaves of the banana plant.

FACT FILE

- **Scientific name:** *Caligo eurilochus*
- **Class:** insect
- **Length:** wingspan up to 5.3 in (13.5 cm)
- **Home:** tropical rainforests
- **Diet:** larvae eat plants, particularly banana plants; adults feed on nectar and juices from fruit

MASTERS OF DISGUISE

Rather like owls, these butterflies fly at dusk. They flit through the rainforests of South and Central America, looking for food. During the day, they rest on a leaf, leaving their wings closed and the eyespots visible. The eyespots protect the butterfly by startling and distracting predators, such as birds. Once a giant owl butterfly reaches its adult phase, it will live for only about seven weeks, during which time it needs to find a mate.

The owl butterfly chrysalis is kept safe from predators by being disguised as a leaf.

The butterfly's eyespots are very realistic with yellow rims and white highlights that look like light reflecting off a pupil.

ALL CHANGE

It's not unusual for insects to look a bit different after each molt, but the giant owl butterfly takes this to extremes. When it first hatches, the caterpillar is white, with red stripes down its back and a furry brown head. The second instar (top right) is green and hairy, with four spines on its back and four pairs of horns on the head. Later instars (bottom right) are brown and up to 6.3 inches (16 cm) long, with six spines on their back.

Each phase of the caterpillar's life lasts only about a week, despite the significant changes.

HERCULES BEETLE

The hero Hercules, from Greek and Roman mythology, was famous for being big and strong. Today, some of the world's largest and strongest insects are named after him! Hercules beetles are found in the rainforests of South and Central America, as well as islands of the Caribbean. They're hugely powerful animals, capable of lifting and carrying objects—and other insects—many times their own body weight.

FACT FILE

- **Scientific name:** genus *Dynastes* (several species)
- **Class:** insect
- **Length:** larvae up to 6 in (15 cm) or more; adult males up to 7 in (17.8 cm)
- **Home:** tropical rainforests
- **Diet:** larvae eat rotting wood; adults eat rotting fruit

SLOW GROWTH

As with many insects, the mature larvae of Hercules beetles are bigger than the adults. Once the eggs hatch, the fat, creamy-yellow larvae burrow into rotting logs and tree trunks to feed on dead wood. They molt twice, getting bigger each time. The first two instar stages last less than two months each, but the third lasts for over a year. After the pupa, which lasts about a month, an adult beetle emerges that can live for several months.

By the time they are ready to pupate, Hercules beetle larvae can be more than 6 inches (15 cm) long and weigh up to 5 oz (140 g).

HERCULES' HORNS

A male Hercules beetle has one long, downward-curving horn on its prothorax (see page 40), and a shorter upward-curving horn on its head. They use these horns to fight with other males when looking for a mate. During a fight, each beetle tries to grab its opponent with its horns, then lift and throw it. The fight ends when one beetle lands on its back, is injured, or gives up and retreats.

The males use their horns like pliers, to grab, squeeze, lift, and toss their opponent to the ground.

LIFE IN THE FOREST

Adult Hercules beetles are nocturnal. During the day, they tend to hide in the carpet of dead leaves on the rainforest floor. At night, they move around looking for overripe fruit that has fallen to the ground. They use their mouthparts to pierce the skin of the fruit, and can also feed on tree sap. Males can make a noise by vibrating their abdomen against their elytra (hard forewings), which might be meant to scare off predators.

Females are smaller than the males, and they don't have horns. Both use their mouthparts to carve tree bark to feed on sap.

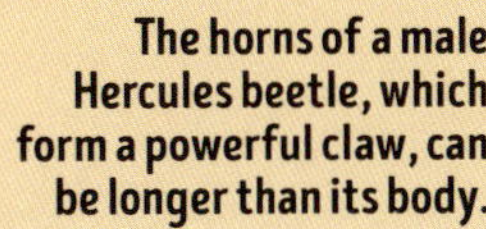

The horns of a male Hercules beetle, which form a powerful claw, can be longer than its body.

STILL LEARNING

Due to their secretive rainforest lives, there is a lot we still need to learn about Hercules beetles. For example, scientists have not yet recorded other animals hunting or eating these beetles. It might be that their horns and sheer size put predators off—but just because we haven't seen it doesn't mean it never happens! In addition, the data we have on the stages of their lifespan was gathered from insects kept in captivity. It might be different for beetles in the wild.

Scientists now know that the beetles' elytra are olive-green in low humidity, but in moist conditions they turn black.

BLUE MORPHO BUTTERFLY

Blue is a fairly rare color among bug species, so the shimmering blue wings of the blue morpho butterfly make it hard to miss. Like most butterflies, these beauties usually rest with their wings closed, leaving only the brown spotted underside showing. But when they take flight, flitting through their rainforest home, their wings open to reveal the iridescent, metallic color of the upper side of the wings.

FACT FILE

- **Scientific name:** genus *Morpho* (several species)
- **Class:** insect
- **Length:** wingspan up to 6 in (15 cm)
- **Home:** tropical rainforests
- **Diet:** caterpillars eat leaves; adults feed on tree sap and juices from fruit

BRILLIANT BLUE

All butterfly wings are covered in scales, which are too tiny to see without a microscope. Yet, the scales on the upper side of a blue morpho's wing are not blue—they're brown! The reason we see them as blue is because of layers of incredibly tiny ridged structures in the scales. When light hits these ridges, they reflect it in such a way that the blue wavelengths of light are intensified.

These scales have been magnified under a microscope. We see the reflection of light as the color blue.

As this blue morpho flies through the forest, you can see the brown coloration of its underside, with glimpses of the bright blue color of its upper side.

FAMILY RESEMBLANCE

Several different—but closely related—butterfly species are known as "blue morphos" because of their blue wings. They each have a slightly different appearance. *Morpho menelaus*, for example, has blue wings edged in black. In *Morpho cypris,* the females are brown and yellow rather than blue. But all the species live in the same kind of environment and have similar life cycles.

This colorful, hairy caterpillar (left) will turn into a *Morpho menelaus* butterfly (right).

KISSING BUG

You'd think that an insect with a name like the "kissing bug" would be cute and cuddly. But that couldn't be further from the truth! These South American bugs like to bite and suck blood from mammals—including humans. They got their nickname because of the belief that they usually bite people around the mouth. However, they can bite anywhere on the body.

FACT FILE

- **Scientific name:** *Triatoma infestans*
- **Class:** insect
- **Length:** up to 1.4 in (3.5 cm)
- **Home:** tropical wooded regions
- **Diet:** blood from mammals

Kissing bugs have a narrow neck and large, bulbous compound eyes. They use their segmented antennae to sense and feel their way around.

SPREADING DISEASE

Kissing bugs spread an illness called Chagas disease. It's caused by a parasite that lives in the bug's guts and comes out in its poop. If the bug poops while feeding, and the person then scratches the bite, this might push the infected poop into the bite. Chagas disease can cause a fever or mild illness, though many people don't have any symptoms at all. However, the parasite remains in the body and can cause heart issues—or other problems—many years later.

This image shows tiny single-celled organisms that cause Chagas disease, seen under a high-powered microscope.

BLOODSUCKERS

Kissing bugs are mainly brown, with yellow or red stripes and spots. Their mouthparts, which include a three-segmented proboscis which they keep tucked under their head, are adapted for piercing skin and sucking blood. The nymphs that hatch from the eggs look similar to adults, and they feed on blood as well. Both nymphs and adults use their antennae to sense the heat of a warm-blooded host.

This artwork shows an engorged kissing bug after a feed. Adults can consume up to eight times their body weight!

ALLIGATOR BUG

This odd-looking bug goes by many different names. To some people it's a lanternfly, while to others it's an alligator bug or a peanut bug. Yet this insect doesn't light up like a lantern, it's not a reptile, and it doesn't eat peanuts. In fact, it isn't even a fly! It's a species of planthopper (see page 134) that lives in the tropical forests of Central and South America.

FACT FILE

- **Scientific name:** *Fulgora laternaria*
- **Class:** insect
- **Length:** body up to 3.5 in (9 cm); wingspan up to 6 in (15 cm)
- **Home:** tropical forests
- **Diet:** plant sap

This alligator bug is resting on a tree in a vertical position. If it wants to attract a mate, it can bang the front of its head on the wood to make a sound.

BIG HEAD

The names "peanut bug" and "alligator bug" both relate to the odd structure that branches off this insect's head. Some people think it looks like a peanut, but when seen from the side, it looks more like the head of a tiny alligator. Both males and females have one, so it's unlikely to be there to attract a mate. It may fool predators into thinking that the bug is a dangerous lizard, or trick them into attacking the wrong part of the insect's body.

Markings that resemble eyes and sharp teeth make the alligator bug's head look even more like its namesake.

KEEPING PROTECTED

During the day, an alligator bug rests on the trunk of a tree, relying on camouflage to keep it safe. If it is disturbed by a potential predator, it might open its wings or display its scary-looking head. An alligator bug can also release a smelly chemical to put off predators. At dusk it begins to feed, using its mouthparts to suck sweet sap from the tree trunks.

The wings of an alligator bug have a pair of eyespots that can scare predators into thinking it's a much larger animal.

LEAFCUTTER ANT

Leafcutter ants are truly fascinating. There are several dozen different species, but they all have similar lifestyles, living in huge colonies and farming food to eat. They're a common sight in the tropical forests of South and Central America, often traveling in single-file lines, each ant carrying a piece of a leaf weighing several times their own body weight.

FACT FILE

- **Scientific name:** *Acromyrmex octospinosus*
- **Class:** insect
- **Length:** up to 0.6 in (1.5 cm)
- **Home:** forests and plantations in tropical regions
- **Diet:** fungus

Leafcutter ants often travel in lines, laying down a chemical trail that will guide them back to the nest. In warmer months, they work at night to avoid high temperatures.

FUNGUS FARMERS

Perhaps surprisingly, leafcutter ants don't actually eat the leaves that they spend so much time collecting. Instead, they take them back to their nest, where they use them to feed a species of fungus that grows there. The ants act as farmers, feeding the fungus and looking after it. In return, they eat a liquid that the fungus produces. It's a relationship that both the ants and the fungus rely on—neither could survive without the other.

The white mass in this image is the life-supporting fungus, shown being tended by leafcutter ants.

WORKING TOGETHER

Leafcutter ants live in huge colonies, often numbering in the millions. Each colony is headed by a queen. The rest of the ants are divided into four main groups, each with a different job. The smallest ants stay in the nest, tending to the fungus. Larger ants go out looking for leaves, accompanied by slightly smaller ants who patrol the area to protect them. The largest ants serve as soldiers. They defend the nest and help to carry bulky items, too.

Leafcutter ants have mandibles that vibrate like chainsaws to help them to cut pieces of leaves, which they then carry back to their nest.

GOLIATH BIRDEATER TARANTULA

Even if you're not usually scared of spiders, the Goliath birdeater tarantula is still the stuff of nightmares. These huge, hairy arachnids are big enough to cover a dinner plate with their legs outstretched. Luckily, they live deep in the rainforests of South America, where there are few people. Despite their name, they rarely eat birds, though they are certainly big enough to.

FACT FILE

- **Scientific name:** *Theraphosa blondi*
- **Class:** arachnid
- **Length:** body up to 5 in (13 cm); leg span up to 11 in (28 cm)
- **Home:** tropical rainforests and marshy areas
- **Diet:** arthropods and small amphibians, reptiles, and mammals

LOOKING FOR LUNCH

Goliath birdeaters are nocturnal, and at night they emerge from their burrows to hunt along the rainforest floor. When they find prey, they sink their 1 inch- (2.5 cm) long fangs into it, injecting a venom that will kill their victim. Chemicals in the venom begin to liquefy the prey's insides as it is dragged back to the spider's burrow. Once there, the tarantula feeds by sucking out the juices.

Goliath birdeaters are big enough to attack and kill small rodents, as well as lizards, frogs, and snakes.

STAY AWAY!

Despite their size, Goliath birdeaters are still in danger from predators such as the coati, a raccoon-like animal that is immune to the spider's venom. As a further defense, the spiders can rub bristles on their legs together to make a hissing noise. And, as a last resort, they can rub their abdomen with their legs to release multiple harpoonlike hairs. Each tiny hair is tipped with stinging barbs that irritate their attacker's eyes and skin.

A Goliath birdeater will often rear up on its hind legs to look big and threatening—a warning that it is about to attack.

THE TARANTULA FAMILY

Goliath birdeaters belong to a larger family of spiders, the tarantulas. Tarantulas are large and usually hairy, and there are species found all over the world. Only the species in the Americas have stinging hairs. Tarantulas can spin webs, but they do not use them for catching food. Instead, they use their webs to line the burrows that they dig in the forest floor.

Jumping spider

Tarantula

The fangs of most spiders face each other, like pincers (top), while the fangs of a tarantula (bottom) point downward.

RECORD-BREAKER

It's official—the Goliath birdeater tarantula holds the Guinness World Record for largest spider ever! The record was set in 1965 when an expedition found a spider with an 11 inch (28 cm) leg span in Venezuela. Decades later, another Goliath birdeater matched its size, but this one was bred in captivity in Scotland. It weighed 6 oz (170 g)—about the same as a medium-sized apple.

The sensitive hairs on a tarantula's legs can detect movement and different smells in the environment.

LEAF-MIMIC KATYDID

The katydids are a large group of insects also known as bush crickets or long-horned grasshoppers. They all have large hind legs and long, thin antennae. There are thousands of species of katydid living in tropical regions around the world. The Amazon rainforest is home to many katydid species that use camouflage to hide from predators, blending in to the foliage by looking exactly like leaves.

FACT FILE

- **Scientific name:** family *Tettigoniidae* (many different species)
- **Class:** insect
- **Length:** up to 6 in (15 cm), depending on the species
- **Home:** often found in tropical forests
- **Diet:** usually plants, though some species eat other insects or small vertebrates

STAYING HIDDEN

Most katydid species are nocturnal. They move about to feed on plants in the dark, when they're less likely to be spotted. Although they have wings, they are not particularly good fliers, though they can jump quickly. To stay safe from predators, such as birds, lizards, spiders, and bats, they rely on their excellent camouflage. Their bodies are adapted to look like the leaves of the plants where they live, so when they're at rest they're hard to spot.

Some katydids look like living leaves, while others have coloration that helps them to imitate a dead leaf on the rainforest floor.

A leaf-mimic katydid's antennae can be longer than its body. These have sensory receptors to help it find its way around, especially at night.

TAKING IT TO EXTREMES

In some species of katydid, the camouflage can be incredibly realistic. Their wings have veins like real leaves do, and many also have spots or patches where the wings are discolored, just like a leaf might be if it was rotting or diseased. The appearance of these katydids sends a message to potential predators, telling them that they're just a rotten leaf that isn't worth eating.

Some katydids have tattered wings that make them look as though they've been nibbled by an ant or a caterpillar.

ORCHID BEE

What color is a bee? It seems like an easy question—they're black and yellow, aren't they? But bees form a very large family of insects, and some branches of their family tree look rather different. Orchid bees are a good example of this. Many of them have bodies that are a shiny, metallic green!

FACT FILE
- **Scientific name:** genus *Euglossa* (several species)
- **Class:** insect
- **Length:** up to 0.6 in (1.5 cm)
- **Home:** forested areas in tropical regions
- **Diet:** nectar, particularly from orchids

Orchid bees are less hairy than most other bee species, with a distinctive metallic sheen. They are known to use their translucent, veined wings to fly long distances in search of particular pollen.

FLOWER FEEDERS

Orchid bees get their name because they feed almost exclusively on the nectar of orchids. Orchids have deep flowers, which would make their nectar hard for most bees to reach. But orchid bees have a particularly long proboscis —long enough to reach deep into the flower to suck up the sugary goodness. As they move from flower to flower, their bodies pick up pollen, helping to pollinate the plants.

An orchid bee's proboscis can be twice the length of its body, helping it to reach the nectar that it needs.

NOT LIKE OTHER BEES

Unlike honeybees, orchid bees do not live in large colonies. Although some species live in small groups, they're not organized in the same way as a honeybee colony. Instead of having queens, workers, and drones (see page 70), all the bees do many different jobs, working individually to build the nest, collect food, and lay eggs. The resulting nest is a cluster of cells that forms a roughly spherical shape.

This artwork shows the cells in an orchid bee nest, which differ from a honeybee nest (see page 71).

WHITE WITCH MOTH

Fluttering through the dusk in the continent's rainforests is a giant white moth known as the white witch moth. It has the largest wingspan of any known moth—when outspread, the wings could stretch the length of a standard 12 inch (30 cm) ruler. Other moth species may have a larger overall wing area, but the white witch moth's wings are longer.

FACT FILE

- **Scientific name:** *Thysania agrippina*
- **Class:** insect
- **Length:** wingspan up to 12 in (30 cm)
- **Home:** tropical rainforests
- **Diet:** unknown; larvae likely eat leaves and adults likely eat nectar or nothing at all

GETTING IT WRONG

In 1705, the German scientist and artist Maria Sibylla Merian published an illustration showing the moth along with its eggs and caterpillar. However, the caterpillar that she shows is from the wrong species. The white witch moth caterpillar remained a mystery until 2020, when a man claimed to have found one. He took care of the caterpillar, which pupated into a white witch moth, and a few years later, another caterpillar of this species was found.

The underside of a white witch moth is dark brown with pale white markings, in stark contrast to the upper side.

MYSTERIOUS MOTH

Perhaps surprisingly, scientists still do not know much about the life cycle of the white witch moth. It's not a rare moth, but its strong wings mean it can travel long distances and its camouflage makes it hard to find. Scientists can make educated guesses, based on what we know of the life cycle of related moth species. It's likely they lay their eggs on a plant that the caterpillars can eat, though scientists don't know which plants, as the few larvae found so far were mature and had already stopped feeding.

The patterns on a white witch moth's wings help it to blend in on lichen-covered tree trunks.

White witch moths rest on tree trunks during the day. The topside of their wings are white with dark speckles.

PATAGONIAN BUMBLEBEE

Bumblebees are a common summer sight in many parts of the world, but there's only one species that lives all the way down on the barren, rugged southern tip of South America. This is the Patagonian bumblebee, sometimes known as the "flying mouse" due to its large size and furry body. It is one of the world's largest species of bumblebee.

FACT FILE

- **Scientific name:** *Bombus dahlbomii*
- **Class:** insect
- **Length:** queens up to 1.6 in (4 cm)
- **Home:** temperate forests and shrubland of southern South America
- **Diet:** nectar and pollen

GENTLE GIANTS

It's not just their large size that sets these bumblebees apart from many of their cousins—they also have a color that's more orange than yellow. They feed from flowers in a range of colors, including red flowers, which many other bee species ignore. Scientists think this is because, while most bees cannot see the color red, the Patagonian bumblebee is able to distinguish it. This makes their role as pollinators even more important.

This bumblebee is covered in pollen from the cardoon, a type of thistle found in South America.

Patagonian bumblebees are often found on purple flowers which are rich in nectar.

UNWANTED INVADERS

The Patagonian bumblebee is under threat from two species of European bumblebee. Both were deliberately imported into Chile to act as pollinators, starting in the 1980s. These other species have now spread into Argentina, where they compete with the Patagonian bumblebee for food. They have also brought unfamiliar diseases that have reduced the number of Patagonian bumblebees even further. The majestic "flying mouse" is now officially classified as endangered.

This European bumblebee is smaller than the Patagonian bumblebee but competes for the same food sources.

EUROPE

Europe is one of the smallest continents, but it still packs in a range of different environments. It stretches from the cold, snowy regions north of the Arctic Circle to the hot and dry Mediterranean coastline. In between these two extremes are tall mountains, ancient forests, and vast grasslands, as well as many wetlands and coastal regions. All of these different landscapes provide a habitat for bugs!

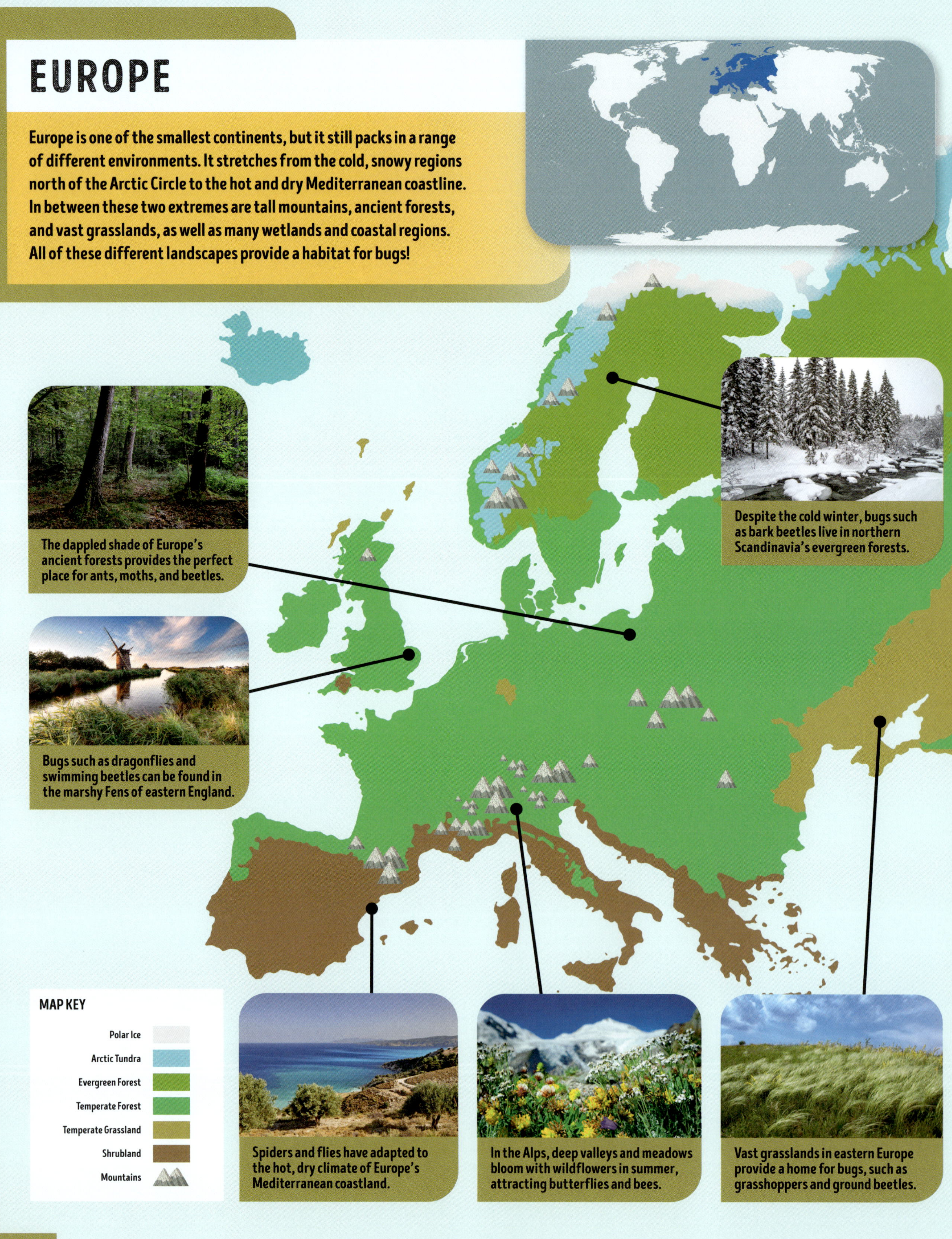

The dappled shade of Europe's ancient forests provides the perfect place for ants, moths, and beetles.

Despite the cold winter, bugs such as bark beetles live in northern Scandinavia's evergreen forests.

Bugs such as dragonflies and swimming beetles can be found in the marshy Fens of eastern England.

Spiders and flies have adapted to the hot, dry climate of Europe's Mediterranean coastland.

In the Alps, deep valleys and meadows bloom with wildflowers in summer, attracting butterflies and bees.

Vast grasslands in eastern Europe provide a home for bugs, such as grasshoppers and ground beetles.

CUCKOO WASP

Shimmering like a colorful Christmas tree ball, the cuckoo wasp looks very different from the yellow-and-black striped pests that plague outdoor diners. Different species of these iridescent, metallic wasps live in many parts of the world. This species is found throughout much of southern Europe, as well as in Switzerland and Poland.

FACT FILE

- **Scientific name:** *Hedychrum rutilans*
- **Class:** insect
- **Length:** adults up to 0.4 in (10 mm)
- **Home:** coastal dunes and other sandy places
- **Diet:** larvae eat other larvae; adults feed on sweet liquid from plants

DAILY LIFE

Cuckoo wasps are solitary and do not form colonies with other members of the same species. They prefer dry conditions and hot temperatures and are mainly active during the summer months. They feed on nectar and plant sap and look for places to lay eggs. When threatened by a predator, they can curl their bodies up into a ball, a bit like a woodlouse does.

This cuckoo wasp is sleeping on the tip of a branch. It has curled up in a ball as a form of defense.

CUCKOO IN THE NEST

Cuckoo wasps get their name because they behave similarly to the cuckoo. This bird is famous for laying its eggs in the nests of other species. The cuckoo wasp does the same, usually targeting a wasp called the beewolf. A beewolf kills honeybees to feed its larvae, and the cuckoo wasp lays its eggs on those bees. When they hatch, the cuckoo wasp larvae eat the honeybee—and the beewolf larvae too!

Cuckoo wasps look for the entrance to a beewolf burrow, then sneak inside to lay their eggs.

The shimmering colors of a cuckoo wasp are caused by layers of tiny structures in its exoskeleton that reflect light.

STAG BEETLE

Stag beetles get their name because they look like they have antlers. However, these "antlers" are actually just a massively enlarged jaw! Like deer, males of this species use these structures to fight with other males when competing for a mate. Although their jaws—or mandibles—look fierce, they're actually quite weak, so they can't bite very hard. But watch out for the females—while their mandibles are much smaller, they can nip hard!

FACT FILE

- **Scientific name:** *Lucanus cervus*
- **Class:** insect
- **Length:** males up to 3 in (7.5 cm), including mandibles
- **Home:** wooded areas in Europe
- **Diet:** larvae eat rotting wood; adults feed on sweet juices from plants

GROWING APPETITE

Most of a stag beetle's life is spent as a larva. It can take four years or more for a beetle to become an adult. Females lay their eggs in dead wood—such as tree stumps or fallen logs—or nearby soil, so when they hatch the larvae will have plenty of rotting wood to eat. They keep eating and growing until they're about the size of a man's thumb. Then they burrow into the soil and go through a fourth molt, turning into a pupa. Once they emerge as adults, they will live for only a few weeks.

Many stag beetle larvae live inside the wood that they eat. They have no need to see, so they are blind.

A female stag beetle (bottom) is much smaller than the male (top), and lacks the male's large mandibles.

OUT IN THE OPEN

Once they have taken their adult form, stag beetles come out to find a mate. The males often stay on trees during the day and fly at dusk. Females tend to stay on the ground. When they find a female, the males often show off by raising and opening their mandibles while they circle around the female. They must be careful though—stag beetles are big enough to make a substantial meal for predators, such as crows, badgers, and foxes.

Stag beetles can fly, but their size and weight make them clumsy in the air.

HOUSE CENTIPEDE

You may have seen one of these little critters scurrying away from you. Despite their name, house centipedes often live outdoors—anywhere that is cool and damp, such as under a rock or in a pile of rotting leaves. But they do come inside buildings too, where they like dark areas, such as cellars or garages, or humid rooms, such as bathrooms. Like all centipedes, they need to stay moist!

FACT FILE

- **Scientific name:** *Scutigera coleoptrata*
- **Class:** myriapod
- **Length:** up to 2.4 in (6 cm)
- **Home:** dark, humid areas, including buildings
- **Diet:** other small arthropods

House centipedes are often found in rotting tree bark because it keeps them camouflaged and is a moist, safe place to hide.

GETTING LEGGY

A house centipede has up to 15 pairs of long, thin legs. When it hatches, it has only four pairs, but each time it molts, it gains more legs. After five molts, it reaches its adult form. These long legs make the centipedes fast runners—they can speed along at up to 1.3 ft (0.4 m) per second, which is more than 6.5 times their body length. If Usain Bolt could do that, he could finish the 100 meters in under eight seconds!

The centipede's hind legs look like antennae, so it's hard for predators to know which end to bite.

FINDING PREY

House centipedes eat worms and snails, as well as cockroaches, fly larvae, spiders, and other arthropods. Although they can see fairly well, they mainly use their antennae, which can smell as well as touch, to find prey. They often jump onto their prey, or sometimes use their legs like lassos to catch it. They inject venom into their prey to kill it before eating it. They will only sting humans if they are threatened, but this is no more harmful than a bee sting.

A house centipede's "fangs" are actually a pair of modified front legs, so they give a sting rather than a bite.

SEVEN-SPOT LADYBUG

Ladybugs are a common sight in parks and gardens, particularly in the summer. Their bright red-and-black coloring makes them easy to spot among leafy, green plants. Ladybugs are a type of beetle, and this species originated in Europe and Asia but has now spread to North America. There are several different species of ladybug, but the seven-spot variety is the most common in Europe.

FACT FILE

- **Scientific name:** *Coccinella septempunctata*
- **Class:** insect
- **Length:** adults up to 0.3 in (8 mm)
- **Home:** any temperate region where plants are found
- **Diet:** other insects, particularly aphids

The "septempunctata" part of the ladybug's scientific name means "seven spots," and most of these ladybugs do have seven black spots.

GROWING UP

When a ladybug larva hatches from its egg, the first thing it does is eat the egg casing. Then it looks for a proper meal! Ladybugs are carnivores that mainly eat aphids (see page 66). As they eat, the young larvae grow and molt. They go through four instars before pupating and changing into their adult form. It takes less than a month for a ladybug larva to go through all these stages and become an adult. The adults can live for one to two years.

A ladybug has laid her yellowy-orange eggs on this plant infested with aphids. When the eggs hatch, there will be plenty of food for the larvae.

DO NOT EAT!

The bright colors of a ladybug, and the markings on their larvae, are a warning to potential predators, such as birds and spiders, that their bodies are toxic to eat. If a predator ignores the warning colors and approaches, the ladybug (or larva) can secrete a foul-tasting toxic liquid. Ladybugs sometimes also play dead to fool predators.

As well as having red warning markings, this aphid-eating larva has bristles and spines along its back that may deter some predators.

SAVING CROPS

Farmers are fans of ladybugs because of the huge numbers of aphids that they eat. Aphids are small insects that feed by sucking out the juices from plants, and in large numbers can cause significant damage to crops. Ladybug larvae start by sucking out the juices from aphids' bodies, before moving on to eat other body parts as well. The adults eat whole aphids, and sometimes pollen and nectar, too.

This ladybug has found an aphid-infested plant to feast on. In one year, an adult ladybug can eat about 5,000 aphids!

FLY AWAY HOME

Ladybugs usually mate in late spring, from May onward. Males will move around, looking for available females. When one finds a potential mate, he feels her antennae and mouth with his own antennae. Once mating has taken place, the female ladybug lays eggs in June and July. She will lay several hundred eggs, usually in small batches. She'll fly from one plant to another to find places to lay her eggs.

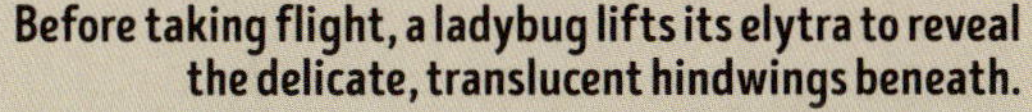

Before taking flight, a ladybug lifts its elytra to reveal the delicate, translucent hindwings beneath.

APPLE APHID

Aphids are a large family of tiny insects with pear-shaped, soft bodies. They all live by sucking the sap from plant leaves and stems, and each individual species tends to specialize in a particular type of plant. The apple aphids live and feed on—you guessed it!—apple trees. They're also often found on closely related fruit trees, such as pear, quince, hawthorn, and medlar.

FACT FILE

- **Scientific name:** *Aphis pomi*
- **Class:** insect
- **Length:** up to 0.1 in (3 mm)
- **Home:** apple trees in temperate regions
- **Diet:** sap from the leaves and shoots of apple trees and other plants

MALES NOT NEEDED?

The way that apple aphids reproduce is fairly unusual in the insect world. Throughout the summer, female aphids give birth to live young instead of laying eggs, and their offspring are all female. They do this without needing to mate. In the fall, female aphids give birth to live males and females. These offspring will mate and produce eggs. The eggs can survive the cold winter and will hatch in the spring. Some female apple aphids have wings, so they can fly to other trees or branches.

This apple tree leaf has been infested with aphids. The aphids particularly like to feed on the underside of young, juicy leaves.

Aphids have infested these apple tree leaves, making them sticky, curled, discolored, and distorted.

APHID INFESTATIONS

Aphids are a real pest for farmers. By sucking sap, aphids often damage the leaves of the plants they feed on, though this does not usually affect the fruit. Aphids also secrete a sugary, sticky substance called honeydew. Black, sooty mold often grows on the honeydew, blocking sunlight from reaching the leaves. Predators, such as ladybugs, lacewings, and hoverflies, feed on aphids, keeping populations under control.

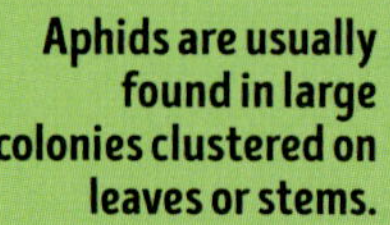

Aphids are usually found in large colonies clustered on leaves or stems.

SOUTHERN WOOD ANT

Europe's temperate forests are home to countless colonies of southern wood ants. These ants live throughout the continent, in both warm and cold locations. They are medium-sized ants with large jaws—or mandibles—which they use to feed on insects and other prey. However, they prefer a different food, which they can get in a much less deadly way...

FACT FILE

- **Scientific name:** *Formica rufa*
- **Class:** insect
- **Length:** workers up to 0.4 in (10 mm); queens up to 0.5 in (1.2 cm)
- **Home:** temperate woodland
- **Diet:** honeydew from aphids; also small insects and arachnids

APHID FARMERS

The favorite food of a southern wood ant is honeydew—not the melon, but rather a sugary liquid produced by the bodies of aphids after they've fed on sweet plant sap. The ants don't want to kill or eat the aphids, because they want them to keep making honeydew. Instead, they tend to the aphids and stroke their abdomens with their antennae. This stimulates the aphids to produce even more honeydew.

WOOD ANT COLONIES

Southern wood ants live in huge colonies that can contain hundreds of thousands of ants. The nests they build are large, dome-shaped mounds made of grass, twigs, and pine tree needles. Inside the nests, they raise their young. They will guard their own nests and territories fiercely, attacking any ants from different colonies. They sometimes also raid the nests of other ant colonies.

This nest has been built around a tree stump, with its tunnels and chambers among the tree roots.

Predators are less likely to attack aphids if there are southern wood ants standing guard over them. The aphids are an important source of honeydew for the ants to eat.

COMMON GREEN GRASSHOPPER

Grasshoppers have been around for a very long time—there were species of grasshopper living during the Triassic Period, over 200 million years ago, alongside some of the earliest dinosaurs. Grasshoppers are usually seen on the grassy plants that they eat, and their strong hind legs allow them to jump long distances to escape predators or find new plants. So there's no prize for guessing how they got their name!

FACT FILE

- **Scientific name:** *Omocestus viridulus*
- **Class:** insect
- **Length:** adults up to 0.9 in (2.3 cm)
- **Home:** meadows and woodlands with long grass
- **Diet:** plants

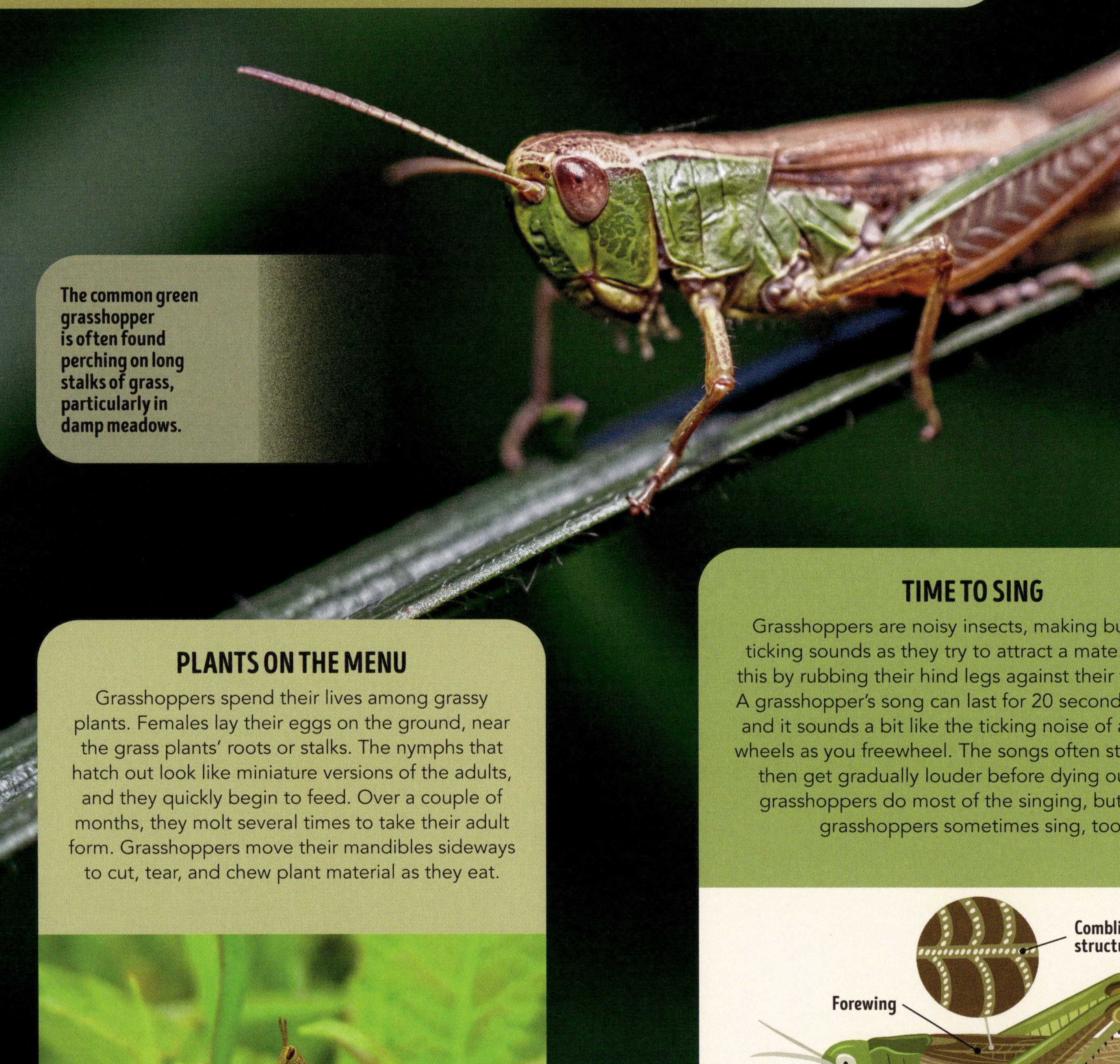

The common green grasshopper is often found perching on long stalks of grass, particularly in damp meadows.

PLANTS ON THE MENU

Grasshoppers spend their lives among grassy plants. Females lay their eggs on the ground, near the grass plants' roots or stalks. The nymphs that hatch out look like miniature versions of the adults, and they quickly begin to feed. Over a couple of months, they molt several times to take their adult form. Grasshoppers move their mandibles sideways to cut, tear, and chew plant material as they eat.

Grasshopper nymphs look more or less like adults, but they do not have working wings.

TIME TO SING

Grasshoppers are noisy insects, making buzzing or ticking sounds as they try to attract a mate. They do this by rubbing their hind legs against their forewings. A grasshopper's song can last for 20 seconds or more, and it sounds a bit like the ticking noise of a bicycle's wheels as you freewheel. The songs often start quietly, then get gradually louder before dying out. Male grasshoppers do most of the singing, but female grasshoppers sometimes sing, too.

Comblike structure
Forewing
Front leg
Middle leg
Hind leg

This artwork shows the comblike structure on the grasshopper's forewing, which it scrapes with its hind leg to produce a sound.

MEADOW FROGHOPPER

FACT FILE

- **Scientific name:** *Philaenus spumarius*
- **Class:** insect
- **Length:** up to 0.3 in (7 mm)
- **Home:** temperate regions
- **Diet:** plant sap

Have you ever gone into a park or garden and noticed what looks like frothy spit on the plants? Chances are, this is the work of a froghopper. These insects are often known as "spittlebugs" because of the foamy "spit" like substance they produce. It may look weird, but it's completely harmless, and just a natural part of this insect's life cycle. The meadow froghopper is found across Europe and into Asia and North America.

BUBBLE-WRAPPED BABIES

Only the young nymphs of froghoppers make froth, sometimes called "cuckoo spit." They drink sugary sap from a plant, then squirt some of it out of their bottoms. Next, they froth it up to make a slippery foam. The foam acts like bubble wrap to protect them from predators, such as ants, and also acts as a barrier to the air, keeping the nymphs' bodies from drying out. Some wasps try to lay their eggs inside a nymph's body, but when the nymph is covered in foam, they can't get a good enough grip.

These nymphs have made their own "cuckoo spit," so-called because it often coincides with the first calls of the cuckoo in spring.

STRONG LEGS

Once the nymphs have grown and taken their adult form, they no longer need to produce spit for protection. They now have another line of defense—their legs! Adult froghoppers have powerful legs and can jump to escape predators. They can clear up to 28 inches (70 cm) in a single leap, which is pretty impressive when you consider that their bodies are less than 0.4 inch (1 cm) long.

This meadow froghopper is resting, holding its wings over its delicate body to protect it from predators. You can see the "beak" at the front of its head, which it uses to drill into plants to find sap.

WESTERN HONEYBEE

The western honeybee is one of the world's most important insects. This species is native to Europe, Africa, and western Asia but, since the 17th century, it has spread or been introduced to every continent except Antarctica. These striped black-and-yellow bees make honey, which we often harvest and eat. But the main way in which they help humans is by pollinating crops and other plants.

FACT FILE

- **Scientific name:** *Apis mellifera*
- **Class:** insect
- **Length:** queens up to 0.8 in (2 cm); drones up to 0.7 in (1.7 cm); workers up to 0.6 in (1.5 cm)
- **Home:** temperate regions with plenty of flowers, such as meadows
- **Diet:** pollen, nectar, and honey

WORKERS, QUEENS, AND DRONES

Honeybees live in large colonies ruled by a single queen. Her job is to lay all the eggs for the colony, so she rarely leaves the hive. The rest of the female bees are called workers. They are not able to lay eggs. Instead, they do all the work for the colony: building the hive, collecting nectar and pollen, and looking after the queen and the young. Male honeybees are called drones. They do not work—their only job is to mate with the queen.

In a bee colony, the queen bee (center) is often surrounded by worker bees. They feed her and keep her clean—just like servants!

Western honeybees are attracted to purple flowers because they can see ultraviolet light and this shade stands out to them. Purple flowers are also often highly scented.

RAISING YOUNG

Worker bees can produce wax from their bodies, and they use it to build honeycomb. This structure has hollow hexagonal cells. A queen bee lays an egg in each cell, and the eggs hatch into little white larvae. The worker bees tend these larvae and feed them, using a special substance produced by glands in their head. The food is a mixture of the pollen and nectar that the worker bee has eaten.

These worker honeybees are tending to larvae in a nest. They have sealed some of the hexagonal cells with wax, so the larvae can pupate into their adult form.

MAKING HONEY

Many of the workers in a bee colony stay busy visiting flowers all day. They use their proboscis to suck up nectar. They also collect pollen, putting it into special "pollen baskets" on their hind legs. Nectar is stored in a special second stomach and turned into a thick, sugary liquid by the addition of enzymes. Back at the hive, the bees regurgitate the nectar into empty cells in the honeycomb, then flap their wings to dry it out. Once sealed into the cell, this honey becomes a store of emergency food.

Some people keep bees to harvest their honey or beeswax. In this beehive, vertically hung frames can be removed to inspect the hive.

POLLINATORS

As worker bees forage for food, their bodies transfer pollen from one plant to another. This is an important part of the process by which plants make seeds and reproduce. Without honeybees, many agricultural crops that we rely on would not get pollinated. Farmers bring bee colonies into their fields to do this job. When insects feed on nectar, it doesn't harm the plants—in fact, plants make nectar solely to attract pollinators like bees!

As a worker bee feeds from a flower, tiny grains of pollen get stuck to her legs and body.

GREAT DIVING BEETLE

It's easy to think that insects all live on land, but in fact many species are adapted for life in the water. The great diving beetle is a large beetle that can swim as well as fly and walk. It lives in bodies of fresh water, where it searches for prey. It's also often found on land, where it can hibernate over the winter, but it relies on ponds and lakes for finding food.

FACT FILE

- **Scientific name:** *Dytiscus marginalis*
- **Class:** insect
- **Length:** larvae up to 2.4 in (6 cm); adults up to 1.4 in (3.5 cm)
- **Home:** freshwater lakes or ponds
- **Diet:** animals including tadpoles and small fish

LIFE UNDERWATER

Great diving beetles lay their eggs underwater in early spring. The larvae that hatch out look a bit like shrimp, with long, thin bodies. They are fierce predators that feed and grow at an impressive rate, molting until they reach a length of about 2.4 inches (6 cm). In late summer, they burrow into the mud along the shore to pupate and take their adult form. As adults, they continue to dive underwater for prey.

The larvae aren't afraid to attack larger prey, such as this tadpole, with their pincerlike mandibles.

BREATHING AIR

Although great diving beetles spend a lot of time underwater, they still need to breathe air. The larvae have special air ducts in their tails, so they often swim with their tail just above the surface. This lets them breathe. Adults store a temporary air supply in a cavity below their forewings. When they need to refill it, they poke their abdomens up above the water's surface to take in more air.

This beetle uses its legs to steer and its hind legs act like oars to push it toward the water's surface to breathe.

The female great diving beetle (left) is smaller than the male (right) and has a series of deep grooves running along her elytra.

HEAD LOUSE

Here's an insect that will really make you itch! The head louse's ideal environment isn't in the outdoors—it's on your head. These tiny creatures live all over the world, anywhere where there are humans with blood to drink. Head lice can only survive without a host for a few days, so they are nearly always found on someone's head. This is where they lay their eggs and live out their lives.

FACT FILE

- **Scientific name:** *Pediculus humanus capitis*
- **Class:** insect
- **Length:** up to 0.08 in (2 mm)
- **Home:** the human scalp
- **Diet:** blood

These head lice are using their claws to crawl between hair strands. They can crawl from one person's head to another if they come into close contact.

FEEDING ON HUMANS

Head lice do not have wings, or strong legs for jumping. Instead, they move about by using their clawlike legs to cling to strands of hair. They crawl around, close to the scalp, and when they get hungry they use their special mouthparts to pierce the skin and suck out blood. They are too small for you to feel them bite you, but their saliva often triggers an allergic reaction that makes your scalp feel itchy.

Medicated shampoos can kill head lice, and a very fine-toothed comb can help to remove them.

NITS AND NYMPHS

Head lice lay each egg on a strand of hair, near the scalp. They tend to prefer locations behind the ears or on the back of the head. The female's body produces a sort of glue that she uses to stick the egg to the hair. The eggs are called "nits," and female head lice can lay three or four eggs every day. The nits take about a week to hatch into nymphs, and another two weeks or so to become adults.

These eggs have become firmly attached to strands of hair with a sticky substance, making them difficult to remove.

HUMMINGBIRD HAWK-MOTH

The hawk-moths are a family of moths that get their name because they can hover in midair, like a hawk does when hunting. Unlike many moth species, the hummingbird hawk-moth is active during the day. Like the hummingbird, it also hovers near flowers in the daytime to suck up nectar with its long proboscis.

FACT FILE

- **Scientific name:** *Macroglossum stellatarum*
- **Class:** insect
- **Length:** caterpillars up to 2.2 in (5.5 cm); adults' wingspan up to 1.8 in (4.5 cm)
- **Home:** temperate areas with plenty of flowers
- **Diet:** caterpillars eat leaves; adults feed on nectar

FEASTING FIRST

A female hummingbird hawk-moth lays her eggs on the buds or flowers of plants such as bedstraw (*Galium*) that provide food for the growing caterpillars when they hatch. After about three weeks of feasting, the caterpillars burrow into loose soil or leaf litter to pupate. The adult moths that emerge have fat, furry bodies, brownish-gray forewings, and orange hindwings rimmed in black. They also have a long proboscis that works like a straw for sucking up nectar.

Hummingbird hawk-moth caterpillars have a harmless horn on their rear end, thought to warn off predators.

MOVING NORTH

Hummingbird hawk-moths like warm climates, and they don't mind foraging even when the temperature tops 104 °F (40 °C). These moths mostly breed in southern Europe and North Africa, where it stays warm all year. In the summer they move north, reaching as far as Scandinavia. In the UK, warmer temperatures due to climate change mean that some hummingbird hawk-moths are staying for the winter, hibernating in garages, porches, and trees.

The proboscis of a hummingbird hawk-moth curls up into a spiral, then unfurls when it is ready to feed.

While hovering, the hummingbird hawk-moth flaps its wings so quickly that it makes an audible humming sound.

COMMON POND SKATER

Have you ever wished you could walk on water? That dream is a reality for the common pond skater. Also known as water striders, these insects are small and light enough to walk on the surface of ponds and lakes. Their strong legs help to distribute their weight over a large surface area, and tiny hairs on their body help to repel water.

FACT FILE

- **Scientific name:** *Gerris lacustris*
- **Class:** insect
- **Length:** body up to 0.4 in (10 mm)
- **Home:** freshwater ponds, lakes, and streams
- **Diet:** insects and other small invertebrates

A pond skater spreads its legs wide to distribute its weight. The surface tension of the water forms a "skin" that is sufficient to hold the insect up.

SPECIAL LEGS

Like all insects, pond skaters have six legs. But in a pond skater, each pair does a different job. The hind legs act as rudders to help it steer, while the middle pair are used like oars to push the pond skater along. The front pair of legs is shorter than the other two, and these legs have claws at the end. The pond skater uses them to sense the vibrations made by prey animals moving around, then grab them for eating.

Once a pond skater has trapped prey, like this cricket, it uses its proboscis to pierce the body and suck up juices.

GROWING HUNTERS

Pond skaters spend the winter sheltering in leaf litter, then come out in the warmer months to breed. The eggs hatch into nymphs that look more or less like the adults. Both nymphs and adults are predators that hunt smaller insects to eat, either on the water's surface or just below it. Pond skaters are fast, traveling at 100 body lengths per second. That's like a human swimming at more than 370 miles per hour (600 kph)!

This nymph will soon become an adult. It takes about a month (four molts) for the nymphs to fully develop.

PEPPERED MOTH

The peppered moth is a medium-sized moth with black-and-white speckled wings, and at first glance it doesn't look like anything special. The males have cool-looking feathery antennae, but these moths don't have flashy colors—they're all about blending in, not standing out. And it's that need to blend in that gives them such a fascinating history. These simple moths show us how evolution works!

FACT FILE

- **Scientific name:** *Biston betularia*
- **Class:** insect
- **Length:** caterpillars up to 2.8 in (7 cm); adults' wingspan up to 2.4 in (6.2 cm)
- **Home:** temperate forests
- **Diet:** caterpillars eat plants; adults do not feed

This peppered moth caterpillar is doing its best twig impression. Can you spot it?

CATERPILLAR CAMOUFLAGE

Peppered moths start to blend in from a very early age. Female moths lay hundreds of tiny eggs in crevices in tree bark in the summer. The caterpillars that hatch out are camouflaged to look like twigs, so they blend in with the trees where they live. Scientists have discovered that the caterpillars can sense a twig's color with their skin and then slowly change their own color to match. The caterpillars munch leaves, grow, and molt. They are fully grown in the fall, and pupate in the ground over the winter to take their adult form.

BLENDING IN

Most peppered moths are white with black speckles. However, some carry a genetic mutation that makes their wings almost black. The lighter-colored moths blend in well on lichen-covered tree trunks, while the black moths are easier for predators, such as birds, to spot. Until a few hundred years ago, fewer of the black moths survived long enough to pass the mutation on to their offspring. This is called natural selection, and it made the black moths much rarer.

This lighter-colored peppered moth is the most common. With its pale wings and dark speckles, it is well camouflaged on light-colored trees.

Over the years, peppered moths have got darker or lighter in color, depending on their environmental conditions.

CHANGING TREES

By the 1800s, the Industrial Revolution was in full swing in the UK. Factories were belching out smoke, and people burned coal to heat their homes. The soot this created settled on tree trunks, making them darker. The black moths now had the upper hand when it came to hiding from predators, and they soon became the most common form in towns and cities. The lighter moths remained common in unpolluted areas of the countryside, where trees were less sooty.

In cities, it took just a few decades for the darker moths (shown here) to outnumber the lighter moths because it was easier for them to stay camouflaged.

BACK TO THE BEGINNING?

By the late 1900s, the British government had passed environmental laws and smoke-spewing factories had cleaned up their act. Less air pollution meant that tree trunks were now less sooty, even in cities. The darker peppered moths were once again at a disadvantage, easily spotted by predators on the lighter tree trunks. Today, the lighter form of the moth is once again the most common in the UK. Scientists have spent a lot of time studying peppered moths, as they show how human activity can affect animal evolution.

This male's feathery antennae have a large surface area, making it easier to pick up the scents of a female nearby.

ANTLION

With many insects, the common name that we use comes from the adult form—for example, the monarch butterfly. But the larvae of the antlion are so fascinating that we use their name for the species in general! The adults have delicate, lacy wings that make them look like dragonflies, but their larvae are anything but dainty. They are fierce predators whose preferred diet of ants gives them the name "antlion."

FACT FILE

- **Scientific name:** *Euroleon nostras*
- **Class:** insect
- **Length:** larvae up to 0.4 in (10 mm); adults' wingspan up to 2.8 in (7 cm)
- **Home:** temperate areas with dry, sandy soil
- **Diet:** larvae eat small arthropods; adults (rarely) feed on plants or small arthropods

An antlion larva's body (seen here magnified) is camouflaged to blend in with stones and sandy soil.

SIT AND WAIT

An antlion lays a trap for its prey by digging a cone-shaped pit in the sand or soil, using its large head to flick sand out of the hole. It then buries itself at the bottom, with only its mandibles sticking out, and waits for prey. It can tell if something is coming by sensing vibrations in the ground. If food is scarce, it will also eat other antlions. In North America, antlion larvae are often known as doodlebugs, because the trails their abdomens leave in the sand look like the doodles a person would make with a pencil.

Once an unlucky insect, such as an ant, slides into the pit, the antlion grabs it and sucks the juices out of its body.

REACHING ADULTHOOD

After about two years of ambushing prey, an antlion larva pupates and changes into an adult. The adults are sometimes called "antlion lacewings" because of their transparent wings. They emerge in late spring and summer but only live for a few weeks. They are also nocturnal, making them harder to spot. They spend their short lives looking for a suitable mate. Once this happens, the female lays eggs in the sand.

Despite their long wings, adult antlions are feeble fliers. Their transparent wings and drab, brown body become a good camouflage against twigs and tree bark.

CRAB SPIDER

It's easy to think that spiders and webs go together like bread and butter. But the truth is that only about half of spider species spin webs to catch prey. Other types of spiders have different ways of catching a meal, and crab spiders are a good example. They rely on camouflage to lie in wait, ready for a meal to come to them. Don't be fooled by the name, though—crab spiders live on flowers, not at the beach!

FACT FILE

- **Scientific name:** *Thomisus onustus*
- **Class:** arachnid
- **Length:** females' body up to 0.4 in (10 mm); males up to 0.2 in (4 mm)
- **Home:** flowers and shrubs in temperate areas
- **Diet:** mainly arthropods; sometimes pollen and nectar

HUNTING TACTICS

Crab spiders get their name because of their crablike body shape and their habit of moving sideways, like a crab. They wait for prey, such as bees, flies, or butterflies, to approach a plant, looking for nectar to drink. When prey comes near, the crab spiders use their long forelegs to grab it, and then subdue it with venom from their fangs. Females can also change the color of their whole body, including the legs.

Male spiders are much smaller than the females and are usually brown or greenish-yellow.

HELPING PLANTS

Pollinators, such as bees, tend to avoid flowers where there are crab spiders, which is hardly surprising! Plants rely on pollinators to help them reproduce, so it seems like crab spiders are hurting plants by keeping pollinators away. However, these very same plants are in danger from other bugs that eat their leaves, petals, and other parts. Crab spiders eat many of these munchers, which helps to protect the plants.

This crab spider is killing a bee—a useful pollinator, but crab spiders also eat bugs that can harm plants.

Female crab spiders like to hide on brightly colored flowers. To blend in, they change their body color to whatever shade of pink, yellow, or white matches best.

PILL WOODLOUSE

Pill bug, roly-poly, sow bug...no matter what you call them, woodlice are fascinating creatures! These little bugs are not insects, arachnids, or myriapods, but crustaceans. So, although they look a bit like short millipedes or caterpillars, they're actually more closely related to crabs and lobsters. They're the only crustaceans that live their lives entirely on land.

FACT FILE

- **Scientific name:** *Armadillidium vulgare*
- **Class:** crustacean
- **Length:** up to 0.7 in (1.8 cm)
- **Home:** temperate woodlands and grasslands, as well as urban areas
- **Diet:** dead plant matter

LITTLE BALLS

This species of woodlouse is often called a "pill bug" or "pill woodlouse" because of its habit of rolling up into a ball—or pill shape—when threatened. In this position, the hard plates on its back protect the softer underside. Its Latin genus name, *Armadillidium*, comes from the armadillo, a mammal that also rolls up into a ball for protection. As a last resort, pill woodlice can also release smelly chemicals to discourage predators.

The pill woodlouse doesn't leave any gap when it rolls up, which offers complete protection.

FORAGING FOR FOOD

Woodlice need a moist environment to keep their bodies from drying out. They often live among leaf litter on the forest floor, where they eat the dead leaves and other plant matter. Sometimes they eat living roots and even weaker individuals from their own species. They also eat their own poop! This is a way of getting nutrients that might not have been fully digested the first time.

Woodlice live and feed on moist, decaying plant matter. When they poop, it helps to recycle nutrients back into the soil.

A pill woodlouse has seven pairs of legs—one pair for each section of its thorax.

PUSS MOTH

The puss moth has two distinct looks: one soft and fluffy, the other bright and scary. The adults of this species have white bodies that are so furry they look like pet cats—which is where the "puss" part of their name comes from. But this is a complete change from what they looked like as caterpillars, with long tail whips and a truly terrifying false face!

FACT FILE

- **Scientific name:** *Cerura vinula*
- **Class:** insect
- **Length:** caterpillars up to 3.1 in (8 cm); adults' wingspan up to 2.8 in (7 cm)
- **Home:** temperate woodlands, gardens, and hedgerows
- **Diet:** caterpillars eat poplar and willow leaves; adults do not eat

CHANGING LOOKS

When they hatch, puss moth caterpillars are small and dark brown, with two long tails that they use to scare predators. They eat, grow, and molt, and, by the time they reach the later instars, these caterpillars are fat and green. They still have the two long tails, which they can wiggle like tentacles, but now they also have a head that looks like a giant red face with two large eyes. Its appearance is enough to scare off many predators, but the caterpillar can also squirt acid at an attacker.

KEEPING PROTECTED

Puss moth caterpillars have strong mandibles, which they use to chew up bark. They mix the bark with silk to create a tough, reinforced cocoon. Inside, they slowly take their adult form during the winter months. The moths emerge in spring, and it's a race to find a mate and lay eggs. The adult moths only live for a week or two. They have no functioning mouthparts, so they cannot eat. They die once they run out of energy.

This tough cocoon, made with bark, protects a puss moth caterpillar while it pupates during the winter.

This male puss moth has feathery antennae for enhanced senses, and its furry body lives up to its namesake.

This puss moth caterpillar is waving its whiplike tail and raising its head to show off its red markings. This is a form of defence.

COCKCHAFER

At first glance, these large beetles may look a bit scary, but cockchafers are completely harmless. In fact, with their unusual antennae and buzzing, clumsy flight, they're actually kind of cute! They're often known as May bugs because the adults emerge in May each year. Some people also call them doodlebugs.

FACT FILE

- **Scientific name:** *Melolontha melolontha*
- **Class:** insect
- **Length:** larvae up to 1.8 in (4.6 cm); adults up to 1.2 in (3 cm)
- **Home:** temperate fields, meadows, grasslands, and wooded areas
- **Diet:** larvae mainly feed on roots; adults feed on leaves and flowers

GROWING UP UNDERGROUND

Female cockchafers use the pointed structure at the end of their abdomen to help lay eggs in soft soil, in batches of about 20. When the eggs hatch, the larvae start to feed on plant roots. They live like this under the soil for three or four years, slowing their development and going into hibernation each winter.

Mature cockchafer larvae can reach the size of an adult's thumb, having spent several years growing underground.

COCKCHAFER PREDATORS

Cockchafer larvae are at risk from moles, which find and eat them as they dig in the soil. Birds also eat the larvae, especially when they're brought to the surface after fields are plowed. If a larva survives long enough to form a pupa, it takes about six weeks to complete its metamorphosis and emerge as an adult beetle. The adults use their antennae to find food and a mate. When they're on the move, they're at risk from hedgehogs and birds, as well as bats.

A cockchafer's antennae open up like the pages of a book to sense their surroundings. Males have seven "leaves" (shown here), while females have six.

BUZZING AROUND

Adult cockchafers make a buzzing, humming noise as they fly around at dusk, looking for a mate or a suitable tree to feed on. The beetles are attracted to light and often bump up against windows. Sometimes, they mistake chimneys for trees and may fall down into the fireplace below, then fly around the house, knocking into things. The cockchafers' buzzing sound led to them being nicknamed "doodlebugs" in the UK. Some of the flying bombs launched against the UK in World War II made a similar buzzing noise, and so they were also called "doodlebugs."

Cockchafers can fly as well as crawl, but they're a bit clumsy in the air due to their size.

Adult cockchafers only live for about six weeks. Much of the time, they keep their antennae closed, as here, but they can open up these fanlike structures to help detect the scents of food or potential mates.

YOUNG PESTS

Although adult cockchafers feed on leaves and flowers, they don't usually eat enough to cause a problem for farmers or gardeners. However, the hungry larvae are a different matter. They live for several years under the soil and, during that time, they can nibble their way through the roots of trees or other plants. Eating the roots damages or kills the plants, and can weaken older trees.

Here, a gardener has caught a cockchafer larva eating and damaging flower bulb roots.

CRANE FLY

Also known as "daddy long legs" in the UK, crane flies are a common sight during the summer. Their slender, gangly bodies make them look like oversized mosquitoes. But they are not closely related to mosquitoes, and they don't suck blood. They don't have a venomous bite, either, despite a popular urban legend that says they're one of the world's most venomous animals.

FACT FILE

- **Scientific name:** *Tipula paludosa*
- **Class:** insect
- **Length:** larvae up to 1.5 in (3.8 cm); adults up to 1.2 in (3 cm)
- **Home:** temperate regions with plenty of plants
- **Diet:** larvae feed on roots or decaying material; adults probably do not eat

KEEPING STABLE

An adult crane fly uses its long legs to keep stable in the air as it flies. It also has clublike halteres which it uses to balance (see page 104). A crane fly's legs are very fragile and often break off if a predator attacks, allowing the crane fly to make a quick escape. Once a leg breaks off, a crane fly cannot regrow it, so it's not at all uncommon to spot one with fewer than six legs.

The halteres are sensory organs that help the crane fly to keep balanced and stable during quick turns or maneuvers.

Adult crane flies have six long, delicate legs, which help them to perch on blades of grass.

LEATHERJACKETS

Female crane flies lay eggs in damp soil. The larvae that hatch out are often known as "leatherjackets." They get this name because of their thick skin. The larvae stay underground for up to a year, nibbling at plant roots—they especially like the roots of grasses. Predators such as hedgehogs, foxes, badgers, and birds eat leatherjackets, digging in the soil to find them.

Leatherjackets eat decaying organic matter so it's good to have a few of these larvae in soil, but a large infestation can cause damage to plants and grasses.

DIVING BELL SPIDER

The vast majority of spider species live on land, while a few venture into the water to find food. But there is only one species that lives almost its entire life underwater—the diving bell spider. These unique spiders can be found in freshwater lakes and ponds across Europe and parts of Asia. Although they must come to the surface to collect air, they have clever ways of taking it underwater to breathe.

FACT FILE

- **Scientific name:** *Argyroneta aquatica*
- **Class:** arachnid
- **Length:** males up to 0.7 in (1.9 cm); females up to 0.5 in (1.3 cm)
- **Home:** freshwater lakes, ponds, and swamps
- **Diet:** small water creatures

This diving bell spider is swimming underwater. The spiders can stay submerged for more than a day.

BREATHING UNDERWATER

Diving bell spiders have special hairs on their abdomen, which capture a bubble of air at the water's surface. Because the spider breathes through its abdomen, it can use this bubble while it's underwater. Diving bell spiders also use their silk to build "diving bells," which they fill with air and then carry underwater. When the oxygen in the diving bell starts to run low, the spider can return to the surface to get more.

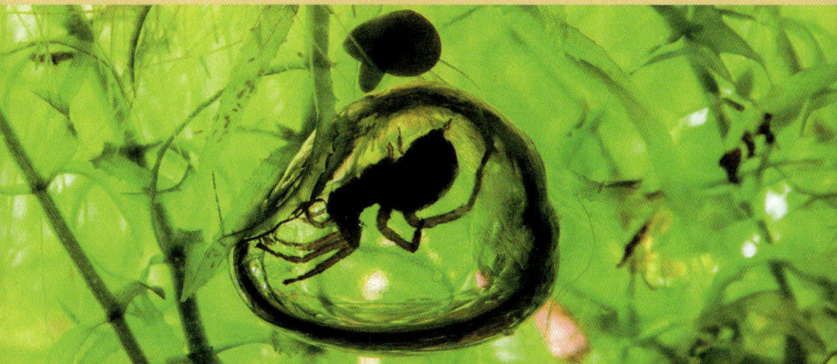

Attached to a plant, this diving bell is like an underwater home filled with breathable air. The spiders stay in these bubbles to eat, molt, mate, and guard their eggs.

CATCHING PREY

Diving bell spiders are predators that eat other small water creatures. Males tend to leave the diving bell to hunt for prey, such as water fleas, tiny shrimp, and insect larvae. Female diving bell spiders spend most of their time inside the diving bell, waiting for prey to come to them. They stick their front legs out into the water below the diving bell and stay alert for vibrations that signal prey is near enough to grab.

This diving bell spider has caught a water louse. It may take it above the water's surface to eat, or back to its air bubble.

AFRICA

When it comes to wildlife, Africa is probably best known for big animals such as elephants, lions, and giraffes, but it is also home to a huge range of smaller creatures—including plenty of bugs! Habitats in Africa range from the arid and barren Sahara Desert to the damp heat of the Congo Rainforest and the vast grassland plains of East Africa. Whatever the environment, there's sure to be a species of bug that has evolved to thrive here.

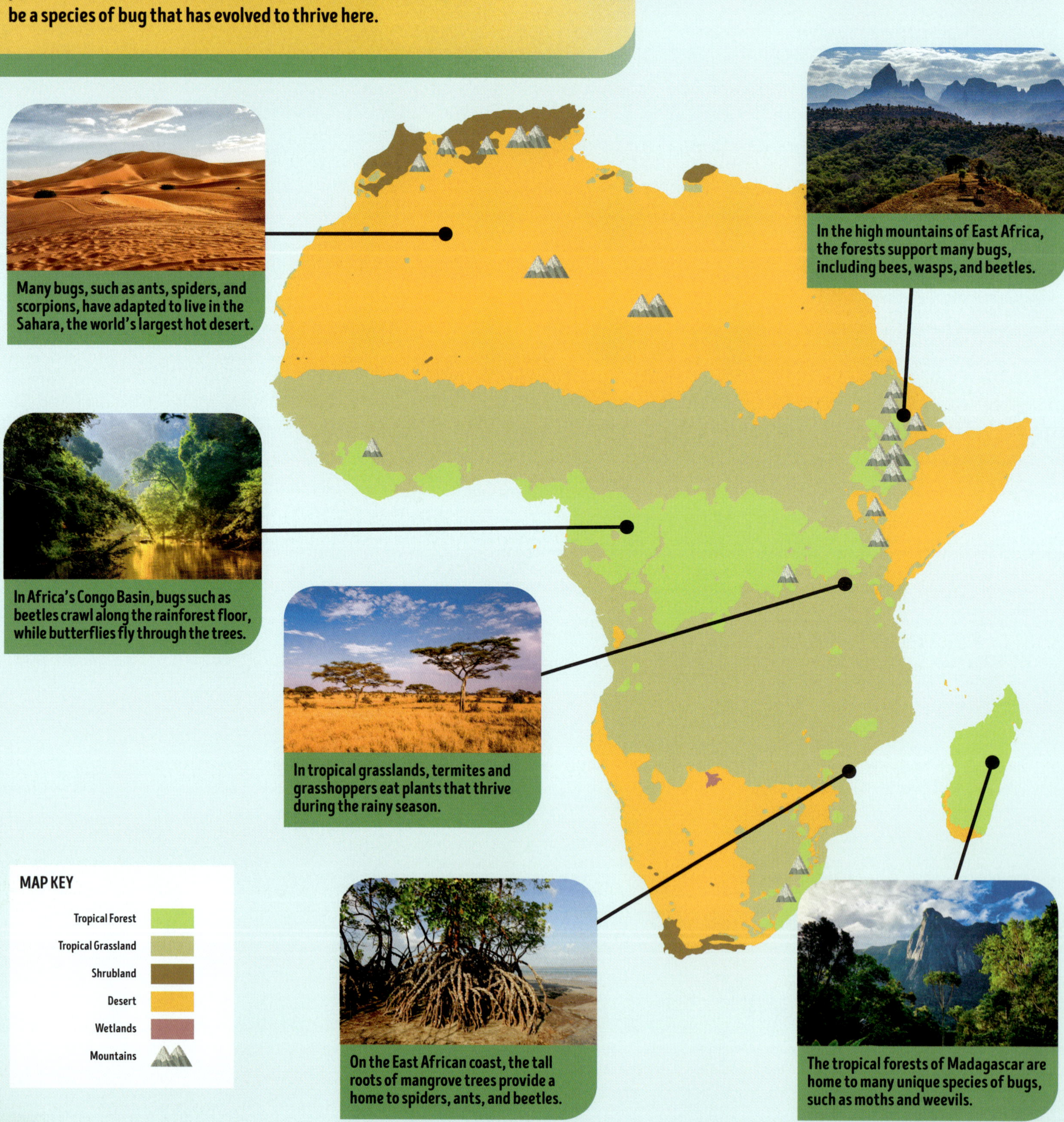

Many bugs, such as ants, spiders, and scorpions, have adapted to live in the Sahara, the world's largest hot desert.

In the high mountains of East Africa, the forests support many bugs, including bees, wasps, and beetles.

In Africa's Congo Basin, bugs such as beetles crawl along the rainforest floor, while butterflies fly through the trees.

In tropical grasslands, termites and grasshoppers eat plants that thrive during the rainy season.

On the East African coast, the tall roots of mangrove trees provide a home to spiders, ants, and beetles.

The tropical forests of Madagascar are home to many unique species of bugs, such as moths and weevils.

GIRAFFE WEEVIL

The huge island of Madagascar lies off Africa's southeastern coast. It's home to many unusual plants and animals that are found nowhere else on Earth. The giraffe weevil might be smaller and less famous than lemurs and chameleons, but it's no less fascinating! This insect gets its name because of its long, giraffe-like neck.

FACT FILE

- **Scientific name:** *Trachelophorus giraffa*
- **Class:** insect
- **Length:** males up to 1 in (2.5 cm); females are smaller
- **Home:** forests in Madagascar
- **Diet:** leaves

LONG AND STRONG

Just as a giraffe's neck allows it to reach leaves on high branches, a giraffe weevil's neck also serves a purpose. The male's neck is about twice the length of the female's. It uses this long neck as a way of showing off to potential mates. It will approach a female and sway its neck in a kind of dance. Males also use their long necks to fight with other males, defending their territory and trying to win the best female to mate with.

Female giraffe weevils have shorter necks than the males, but their necks are still strong and can be used to roll leaves (see right).

LEAF ROLLERS

Giraffe weevils spend most of their lives on a species of tree known as the "giraffe beetle tree." When the female lays an egg, she uses her strong neck and legs to make a leaf "cradle" to protect it. She bends and rolls up a leaf into a secure tube, then bites the edge of the leaf to detach it from the tree, and the tube lands softly on the forest floor.

This leaf "cradle" will have a single egg inside. When the egg hatches, the larva can eat the leaf cradle.

A giraffe weevil's black body and bright red elytra make it stand out from the forest leaves. Giraffe weevils can fly if they need to find food or escape from predators.

RAINBOW SHIELD BUG

Considered by many as one of Earth's most beautiful bugs, the rainbow shield bug gets its name from the dazzling array of colors reflected by its iridescent exoskeleton. Native to the subtropical woodland of Southern Africa, it has also adapted to tropical regions in Asia. These creatures use their piercing and sucking mouthparts to feed on seed capsules and young saplings.

FACT FILE

- **Scientific name:** *Calidea dregii*
- **Class:** insect
- **Length:** up to 0.6 in (1.5 cm)
- **Home:** tropical woodland and farmland
- **Diet:** sap from seed capsules, flowerheads, and young buds

Rainbow shield bugs have a metallic sheen to their body and a yellowish-pink underside, to deter predators.

CLOSE PROTECTION

The rainbow shield bug has a platelike shield protecting its body. It may be a beauty, but its colors are a warning for predators to stay away. Two glands near its hind legs release a foul-smelling odor if anything gets too close. Adults only live for around two months, but the females lay eggs every five days. Some of these eggs are eaten by nymphs and adult shield bugs, but plenty survive into adulthood.

Smaller than an adult fingernail, rainbow shield bugs can be found on vegetation or scurrying in soil.

FARMERS' FURY

For farmers, the rainbow shield bug is a menace! Their feasting habits can affect seed development, reducing crop quality or quantity. In particular, the bugs have affected sunflowers, *Jatropha* plants (used for the biofuel industry), and are known to stain cotton, reducing the quality of the harvest. Farmers have tried to plant their crops earlier in the season to avoid infestation, or to plant 'trap crops' that are more likely to attract the pests.

Pure white cotton bolls can be stained brown or black by a rainbow shield bug infestation, reducing the crop's value in the marketplace.

GOLIATH BEETLE

Some of the largest and heaviest insects on Earth, Goliath beetles are incredibly strong as well as striking looking. Named after Goliath, a giant described in the Bible, they are almost the size of a human hand. Native to different parts of Africa, they use their strength to fight, dig, and carry food. They are also skilled and agile climbers.

FACT FILE

- **Scientific name:** genus *Goliathus* (several species)
- **Class:** insect
- **Length:** up to 4.3 in (11 cm)
- **Home:** trees and burrows in tropical forests
- **Diet:** larvae eat rotting wood and insect larvae; adults feed on tree sap and ripe fruit

Adult male Goliath beetles have Y-shaped horns which they use for fighting, and their sharp claws act like crampons on rough tree bark.

GREAT APPETITE

Adult Goliath beetles have a sweet tooth, preferring to feast on ripe fruit, nectar, and tree sap. Their larvae eat rotting wood as well as other insect larvae and pupae in the soil. The adults scurry around on the ground but can also climb trees and vines. They don't hang around though—they're far too heavy to perch on a leaf! Despite their weight, the beetles can fly short distances, to search for food or a mate.

As this artwork shows, adults have a pair of elytra (hard forewings) which act as a protective cover for their delicate hindwings and abdomen.

Goliath beetles weigh the most during their larval stage, up to 3.5 oz (100 g). This image shows the size on a tablespoon. Adults weigh half this amount.

MADAGASCAN SUNSET MOTH

Many people mistake this moth for a butterfly, and it's not hard to see why. There's a common belief that all moths are dull-colored and only come out at night. But this moth flies around the forests of Madagascar during the day, shimmering with rainbow colors! Like a number of other moth species, it seems to break the rules.

FACT FILE

- **Scientific name:** *Chrysiridia rhipheus*
- **Class:** insect
- **Length:** caterpillars around 2.3 in (6 cm); adults' wingspan up to 3.5 in (9 cm)
- **Home:** deciduous forests of Madagascar
- **Diet:** larvae feed on leaves; adults feed on nectar

WHAT'S THE DIFFERENCE?

It's actually a myth that all butterflies have bright colors while moths are dull—there are some bright moths and plenty of dull-colored butterflies. There are also lots of moths, like the Madagascan sunset moth, that are busy during the day. The main differences are that butterflies usually have club-shaped antennae, while most moths' antennae are either threadlike or feathery. Butterflies usually rest with their wings folded upward and pressed together, while moths keep theirs alongside the body. However, there are exceptions even to these rules!

The sunset moth was once classed as a butterfly, but this female has threadlike (rather than clublike) antennae.

The vibrant colors of the Madagascan sunset moth are breathtaking. Its scientific name *Chrysiridia* comes from Greek words meaning "gold" and "rainbow."

The tiny wing scales of the Madagascan sunset moth can be seen under a high-powered microscope. Their structure affects which colors of light are reflected, and how.

SHIMMERING WINGS

A Madagascan sunset moth's most striking feature is its brightly colored wings, which warn predators that it is toxic. Their metallic shimmer is called iridescence, and even the undersides of the wings are like this! The black color of parts of the wings is caused by pigments, but the rainbow colors are created in a different way. Microscopic structures interfere with the way that light is reflected, resulting in a rainbow of colors.

TOXIC DIET

Madagascan sunset moths are quite picky about where they lay their eggs—they use only the leaves of plants known as *Omphalea*. When the eggs hatch, these plants are what the caterpillars will feed on. They have been known to eat the whole plant, including the flowers and fruit! They take in toxins from the plant, which makes their bodies toxic to most predators. The caterpillars are white with black speckles, and covered in tall black bristles.

The sunset moth caterpillar spins silk from its mouth (shown here on the right), to help stay attached to a smooth leaf.

LOOKING FOR NECTAR

Once the caterpillars have turned into moths, they fly through the forest looking for flowers to feed on. Madagascan sunset moths feed on nectar from a range of different plants. They no longer feed on toxic *Omphalea* plants, but their bodies keep the toxins from their caterpillar stage. However, a few predators, such as chameleons and some bird species, are able to eat them because their bodies can tolerate the toxins.

Sunset moths are often attracted to flowers that give easy access to the nectar they contain.

AFRICAN FLOWER BEETLE

With a shiny, iridescent color, these beautiful beetles are sometimes known as "gemstones with legs." They live in the rainforests of Central Africa and are part of the same large family that includes dung beetles (see page 102). They're also related to rhinoceros beetles, Hercules beetles (page 48), and Goliath beetles (page 89), but are much smaller, only reaching about 0.9 inch (2.4 cm) in length.

FACT FILE

- **Scientific name:** *Chlorocala africana*
- **Class:** insect
- **Length:** up to 0.9 in (2.4 cm)
- **Home:** tropical rainforests
- **Diet:** larvae eat rotting wood and leaf litter; adults feed on flowers, fruit, and plant sap

The African flower beetle comes in a range of colors—green is most common, but they can also be red, purple, or deep blue.

PICK AND MIX

African flower beetles are also related to cockchafers (see page 82), and they're sometimes known as flower chafers. Their range of colors shimmer with a metallic iridescence. In the past, the different color variations led scientists to describe them as different subspecies, dependent on a particular location. However, the differences are now thought to be color variations of the species with no geographical significance.

In sunlight, the beetle's metallic sheen is even brighter. Flower beetles are popular with collectors and are often kept as pets.

FINDING FOOD

African flower beetles have fat, cream-colored larvae. They live on the rainforest floor, eating dead plant material and rotting wood. Once they take their adult form, they look for different food, such as sap or rotting fruit. The beetles are good fliers, capable of quick takeoffs and steady hovering. They sometimes escape predators by "falling" off a plant and then unfolding their wings and flying away just before they hit the ground.

The adult beetles can fly from plant to plant, looking for flower nectar, pollen, and plant sap.

WASP SPIDER

The black, yellow, and white stripes on this spider's large abdomen make it look a bit like a wasp and give it its common name. That resemblance is enough to keep many predators away, not wanting to get stung! These spiders are venomous, but they are not aggressive or dangerous to humans. They are found in North Africa as well as Europe and the Middle East.

FACT FILE

- **Scientific name:** *Argiope bruennichi*
- **Class:** arachnid
- **Length:** males up to 0.2 in (6 mm) body length; females up to 0.8 in (20 mm)
- **Home:** mainly grasslands and meadows
- **Diet:** other arthropods

SPINNING WEBS

Wasp spiders are orb-weaver spiders, meaning that they spin spiral-shaped webs. They tend to build their webs in long grass, low to the ground. These webs often have a stripe down the middle made of thicker silk arranged in a zigzag pattern, though scientists haven't agreed on what this might be for. When prey gets trapped on the web's sticky silk, the spider wraps it in more silk and then bites its prey to paralyze it and dissolve its insides.

DANGEROUS MATING

Like many other spider species, the male wasp spiders are much smaller than the females. What's more, the females have a habit of eating their partners once mating is finished. Some males try to avoid this by waiting at the edge of the web until a female has completed her final molt. After the molt, the female's chelicerae (jaws) will be softer for a short time, making it harder for her to eat him.

This male wasp spider (top) is in danger—a female often eats her partner after mating, using the protein to help grow her eggs.

This female wasp spider has wrapped her prey in silk. Some scientists think the zigzag stripe may strengthen the web or be used to attract prey, such as flies and crickets, as it glistens in the sunlight.

EMPEROR SCORPION

Emperors rule over vast empires, so it's not surprising that the emperor scorpion is one of the largest scorpions in the world! They live in West and Central Africa, burrowing into the leaf litter found in hot, humid forests. Although they look fierce, they're actually quite timid and their sting is fairly mild compared to that of other scorpions. This makes them popular as pets.

FACT FILE

- **Scientific name:** *Pandinus imperator*
- **Class:** arachnid
- **Length:** up to 7.8 in (20 cm)
- **Home:** hot, humid forests of West and Central Africa
- **Diet:** small arthropods and other animals

YOUNG SCORPIONS

Scorpions are unusual among arthropods because they give birth to live young instead of laying eggs. When the juveniles are born, they look like miniature versions of their parents, but their exoskeletons are still soft and light-colored. As they grow, their exoskeleton will harden and darken. Until this happens, the young ride around on their mother's back for safety.

This emperor scorpion is carrying her young on her back. It will take about three weeks for their exoskeletons to harden.

STINGERS AND PINCERS

Emperor scorpions share their environment with termites, and they often burrow deep into termite mounds to eat the insects within. Younger scorpions use the stinger at the end of their tail to inject prey with paralyzing venom. The venom also liquefies the creature's insides, making them easier to suck out. Adult scorpions don't use their stinger as much—they prefer to use their large pincers to grab prey and tear it apart.

Emperor scorpions will eat anything they can catch, including insects like this cockroach, and small rodents.

Emperor scorpions look scary but they are perfectly safe for humans. They are often used in films and television for this reason.

VIOLET DROPWING

The beautiful violet dropwing is a species of dragonfly found throughout most of Africa. It's part of a smaller group within the dragonflies that are known as dropwings because once they land on a perch, they immediately lower their wings. The violet dropwing is also found in many parts of the Middle East, and it is spreading into southern Europe.

FACT FILE

- **Scientific name:** *Trithemis annulata*
- **Class:** insect
- **Length:** wingspan up to 2.4 in (6 cm)
- **Home:** warm regions near fresh water
- **Diet:** larvae eat tadpoles, small fish, and aquatic insects; adults feed on small flying insects

LIFE NEAR THE WATER

Violet dropwings are often seen perched on a twig or reed near a body of fresh water during the day. The female lays her eggs on aquatic plants, or lays them directly into the water by flying and dipping the tip of her abdomen in the water to release the eggs. When the nymphs hatch, they live in the water and hunt for prey, such as tadpoles or small fish. Nymphs only emerge from the water when they're ready to take their adult form, and this can take a few years. Once they're adults, they fly rather than swim to find food.

With her drab coloring, the female violet dropwing stands out less than the male. She'll lay hundreds of eggs during her adult life, so this camouflage is useful.

HUNTING ON THE WING

Violet dropwings have large compound eyes. Their eyesight is excellent, and they can see around 200 images per second. As humans, we see about 30–60 images per second, so for a dragonfly everything appears to be in slow motion. This excellent eyesight, combined with their agile flying skills, helps them as they hunt. They snatch prey, such as flies and mosquitoes, out of the air, using their legs to hold and carry their meal.

A male violet dropwing's huge, colorful eyes dominate its face. These eyes capture a great deal of light for excellent all-around vision.

The male violet dropwing has a particularly striking violet-red color, with red veins on its wings.

FOG-BASKING BEETLE

Deserts can be difficult places to survive. They're dry and often very hot during the day, and little plant life grows there. Animals that live in deserts must have adaptations that help them to get the most out of these harsh habitats. The fog-basking beetle, which lives in the Namib Desert of southwestern Africa, has a unique way of getting a drink. Instead of finding pools of water, it makes use of the fog that often blows in from the ocean.

FACT FILE

- **Scientific name:** *Onymacris unguicularis*
- **Class:** insect
- **Length:** body up to 0.8 in (2 cm)
- **Home:** Namib Desert, southwest Africa
- **Diet:** decaying plant and animal matter

DOING HANDSTANDS

In the Namib Desert, dawn often brings thick fog, which rolls in from the sea over the tops of the tall sand dunes. When this happens, the beetles climb the dunes and stick their abdomens up into the air, like doing a handstand. Fog condenses in tiny droplets on their body. Once enough of these tiny drops stick together, they trickle down through grooves in the wing cases and into the beetle's mouth.

This artwork shows the beetle's stance when drinking. Keeping its back end in the air allows the droplets to run toward its mouth.

LIFE ON THE DUNES

Fog-basking beetles are not picky about what they eat, which helps them to survive in an environment where food is scarce. During the day they forage for tiny particles of decaying plant and animal matter that they find in the sand. Most of this has blown in on the winds that sweep the desert landscape.

Fog-basking beetle larvae burrow to find patches of damp sand to absorb the water. They look like segmented white caterpillars.

This fog-basking beetle has climbed a sand dune. Here, fog-laden winds sweep in from the ocean and condense as water droplets on the beetle's body.

RED VELVET MITE

There are many different species of mite known as red velvet mites—hundreds of them, in fact! They all belong to the same family, and they get their name because their red bodies are covered in tiny hairs that give them a velvety appearance. Different species of red velvet mite live all over the world, and many of them make their home in Africa.

FACT FILE

- **Scientific name:** family *Trombidiidae* (many different species)
- **Class:** arachnid
- **Length:** many less than 0.2 in (4 mm); a few species up to 0.4 in (10 mm)
- **Home:** many different habitats
- **Diet:** larvae drink blood; adults eat insect eggs and very small animals

A red velvet mite's bright color warns predators that it is toxic, while the claws at the end of its legs offer a good grip on vegetation.

MIGHTY MITES

Like all other mites, red velvet mites are arachnids, and their relatives include spiders and ticks. They have eight legs, with a simple body shape that is not divided into segments like an insect's. All mites are very small, but a few species of red velvet mite are quite a bit larger than the others —though still barely 0.4 inch (1 cm) long.

Red velvet mites are often seen in gardens. They like to hang out in wood and plant litter but can also be seen on flowers and on paths and paving.

YOUNG HITCHHIKERS

A red velvet mite's life cycle starts as an egg, then as a tiny creature known as a pre-larva before it becomes a larva. Larvae have six legs rather than eight. To feed, they must climb onto the body of another arthropod, such as a grasshopper or spider. There, they pierce their host's exoskeleton and suck its blood. Eventually, they move through several nymph stages and become adults.

These red velvet mite larvae have hitched a ride on the back of a grasshopper, sucking its blood as they grow.

PICASSO BUG

Anyone who has seen the brightly colored Cubist paintings of the Spanish artist Pablo Picasso will understand how this little insect gets its nickname. The "shield" that forms its back is decorated with eleven ring-shaped spots arranged in a symmetrical pattern. The pattern looks beautiful enough to have been painted on, but it's completely natural.

FACT FILE

- **Scientific name:** *Sphaerocoris annulus*
- **Class:** insect
- **Length:** up to 0.6 in (1.5 cm)
- **Home:** tropical regions of Africa
- **Diet:** plants

The unusual pattern on a Picasso bug serves as a message to potential predators, telling them to stay away.

CROP EATERS

Picasso bugs start their lives as nymphs. The nymphs are a similar shape to the adults, but they are creamy-white with black stripes and spots. They don't get their more colorful turquoise-and-orange pattern until they reach their adult form. Both adults and nymphs feed on plants by sucking out their juices. They often feed on farmers' crops, sometimes damaging the host plant. Picasso bugs are regularly found on coffee plants, citrus trees, and okra plants.

Picasso bugs inject their saliva into plants, which makes them soft and runny. Then they suck up the juices.

USEFUL STINK

When threatened, Picasso bugs can release a smelly chemical. It comes from glands along the sides of the thorax. This smell is enough to deter many predators, especially when lots of Picasso bugs are in the same area. By working together, they can produce a really powerful stench! There is also safety in numbers, as it means more potential targets for a predator—so an individual bug has a better chance of escaping.

Picasso bugs are not strong fliers but they can fly in short bursts, or confuse predators by dropping to the ground.

TSETSE

These African flies are more than just a nuisance—they can be deadly. The bite of an infected tsetse can pass on tiny single-celled organisms that cause a dangerous disease known as sleeping sickness. Tsetses are bloodsuckers that feed on mammals, such as cattle, antelope, pigs, warthogs, and humans. They are found across Central and West Africa, living in grasslands during the wet season and moving into shady wooded areas in the dry season.

FACT FILE

- **Scientific name:** *Glossina morsitans*
- **Class:** insect
- **Length:** up to 0.5 in (1.4 cm)
- **Home:** tropical grasslands and woodland
- **Diet:** blood

The tsetse has a needlelike proboscis which is protected by palps on either side (like a protective sheath), when it's not feeding.

DANGEROUS BITE

Tsetses find host animals by smelling scents such as the carbon dioxide they breathe out. Then they land and use their mouthparts to pierce the skin to suck up blood. This is how they pass on the organism that causes sleeping sickness. People in areas where tsetses live set up traps for them. They hang flags sprayed with insecticide and use cow urine to attract the flies, because they mistake it for the smell of a host. When flies land on the flag, the insecticide in the fabric kills them.

Tsetse traps are blue and black because tsetse flies are attracted to the color blue and seek out dark, shadowy places to land and rest.

BIRTHING YOUNG

Tsetses have an unusual life cycle. In most insects—including most species of fly—the females lay eggs. However, tsetses give birth to live larvae! A female can only produce one larva at a time. The larva goes through its first two molts while still inside her body. A gland in her abdomen produces a milky substance to feed it. Once she gives birth, the larva burrows into loose soil and pupates. It takes about a month to turn into an adult.

This tsetse fly is giving birth to a larva. By the time it's born, a larva is nearly the size of an adult fly.

MOPANE WORM

Despite their name, mopane worms are not worms at all! They're actually caterpillars—the larvae of a species of emperor moth. They get their name because they're usually found on the mopane tree, a type of tree that grows in Southern Africa. These caterpillars also eat the leaves of other trees, such as mango trees, which can often be found in the same area as mopane trees.

FACT FILE

- **Scientific name:** *Gonimbrasia belina*
- **Class:** insect
- **Length:** larvae up to 3.1 in (8 cm); adults' wingspan up to 6 in (15 cm)
- **Home:** wooded and grassland areas of Southern Africa
- **Diet:** larvae eat leaves; adults do not eat

Mopane worms start off light brown but they soon turn black, peppered with spots of white, yellow, and red.

FROM CATERPILLAR TO MOTH

Mopane worms feed on the leaves of the tree where they hatched in the summer. They eat a lot and grow rapidly, molting four times within about a month. Their fifth instar crawls down from the tree and digs into the ground to pupate. The pupa stays underground for at least six months over the winter. The moths that emerge at the beginning of spring only live for a few days, which they spend trying to find a mate.

The moths are light brown, with black-rimmed orange eyespots on the hindwings to deter predators like woodland birds.

EDIBLE INSECTS

Mopane worms have become an important food for many people in Southern Africa. They're a cheap, reliable, and sustainable source of protein. People usually harvest the caterpillars during their fifth instar, when they are biggest. If the caterpillars are found in trees, they must be squeezed like a tube of toothpaste to get rid of their guts, which aren't good to eat. The caterpillars are found in large numbers, and one person can collect many kilograms per day.

These mopane worms are being sold at a market. The worms have been boiled, salted, and sun-dried or smoked. Tinned worms are also sold in supermarkets.

AFRICAN FRUIT BEETLE

This large, green and yellow beetle is a common sight in the rainforests of Africa, and can be about the length of your finger. It's known as the fruit beetle because the adult beetles feed on fruit and plant sap. Because of its large size and colorful appearance, it's often also called the magnificent fruit beetle.

FACT FILE

- **Scientific name:** *Mecynorhina polyphemus*
- **Class:** insect
- **Length:** males up to 2.8 in (7 cm)
- **Home:** dense African rainforests
- **Diet:** larvae eat rotting plant material; adults feed on fruit and plant sap

STEADY GROWTH

Fruit beetles lay their eggs in the damp soil on the forest floor where they hatch into tiny white larvae. These larvae feed on rotting wood and dead leaves and grow quickly, molting each time they outgrow their exoskeleton. When the larva is ready to pupate, it builds an oval-shaped cocoon made of silk and organic matter and attaches it to a solid surface. Inside, it takes its adult form. Once the beetle emerges, it will live for several months.

It takes about four months for a fruit beetle larva to reach its full size, as shown here, before it pupates.

The African fruit beetle's thorax is green with parallel yellow lines. The elytra are the same green color, but instead of stripes they have yellow spots arranged in rows.

BODY FEATURES

Male African fruit beetles have a Y-shaped "antler" on their head. They use this to fight other males to compete for a mate. The beetles with the most prominent horns are regarded as the strongest. Females don't have this horn, but they have a shovel-shaped head that they can use to navigate the rainforest floor and burrow into fruit. Their spiky front limbs are also good for navigating rough terrain.

The female fruit beetle (left) is shinier than the male, while the male's elytra are more water-resistant—although scientists don't know why yet.

DUNG BEETLE

Many different animals eat poop, but only dung beetles take so much effort to prepare it! These beetles often roll the dung into neat round balls and take it back home with them. There are many species of dung beetle found all over the world, but those in the genus *Scarabaeus* live in Africa, with some species also found in parts of Europe and Asia.

FACT FILE

- **Scientific name:** genus *Scarabaeus* (many species)
- **Class:** insect
- **Length:** up to 1.2 in (3 cm), depending on the species
- **Home:** desert, grassland, or forest, depending on the species
- **Diet:** mainly dung; also decaying plant matter

DELICIOUS DUNG

Animal dung is full of nutrients from undigested food, which is why dung beetles eat it. It provides all the nutrition and water that they need, and a large ball of dung can provide food for days. Dung beetles usually bury their dung balls in the soil. This keeps them from drying out and becoming too hard to eat. Dung beetles also lay their eggs in balls of dung. When they hatch, the larvae will have plenty of food!

These dung beetles have found a plentiful supply of dung to roll up and take away as a food store.

Dung beetles sometimes work together to steer, lift, and push the dung balls, to overcome the challenges of rough terrain.

ROLLING BALLS

When they find a fresh source of dung, dung beetles use their head and front legs to roll it into a round ball. Once the ball is finished, it's time to push it back home. The beetles balance and walk on their front legs with their abdomen up in the air, using their hind legs to push the ball along. Even walking backward on only two legs, they can still roll a ball of dung many times larger than themselves!

In many species, the powerful front legs (left) have spikes to help dig, gather, and roll dung, while the back legs (right) are also useful for pushing.

SACRED SCARABS

One species of dung beetle, *Scarabaeus sacer*, was sacred to the ancient Egyptians. To them, dung beetles were linked to Khepri, the god of the rising Sun. Every day, Khepri pushed the Sun across the sky—similar to the way that dung beetles roll round, Sun-shaped dung balls. The ancient Egyptians often wore protective jewelery shaped like scarabs, which they believed kept them from harm.

In ancient Egypt, dung beetles were carved in stone artwork as symbols of regeneration and rebirth.

FINDING THEIR WAY

When rolling their balls, dung beetles have an amazing ability to find their way. One species, *Scarabaeus satyrus*, prefers to roll its balls at night, but still manages to stay on course. Scientists already knew that some animals use the position of the Moon to navigate, but a team of researchers was surprised to learn that these beetles could find their way even on moonless nights! They did some experiments and discovered that the beetles use the Milky Way to orient themselves.

The Milky Way forms a band of light across the sky that dung beetles can use to guide themselves around.

YELLOW FEVER MOSQUITO

This insect originated in Africa but has since spread to warm climates around the world. Mosquitoes are a type of fly. Like their relatives, they have a single pair of wings but are very agile fliers. Mosquitoes and other flies have a pair of tiny, club-shaped organs called halteres (see page 84), which provide information on body position and help them to perform acrobatics in the air.

FACT FILE

- **Scientific name:** *Aedes aegypti*
- **Class:** insect
- **Length:** up to 0.3 in (7 mm) long
- **Home:** warm regions near standing water
- **Diet:** larvae eat microorganisms; adults feed on plants or blood

TIME FOR A MEAL

Mosquitoes are best known for biting humans and drinking blood, but only adult females do this. Adult males, which are smaller, feed on plant juices, nectar, and fruit. And the larvae eat something else entirely! Mosquitoes lay their eggs in water, and when they hatch the larvae remain there, eating tiny organisms such as algae and bacteria. They are sometimes known as "wrigglers" because when they're disturbed, they wriggle downward in the water.

These mosquito larva are "hanging" from the surface of the water, which allows them to breathe air through tubes at the end of their abdomen.

SPREADING DISEASE

Many species of mosquito spread disease when they bite humans, and the yellow fever mosquito is no different. In addition to spreading yellow fever, this species also passes on dozens of other viruses, including those that cause Dengue fever and Zika fever. A mosquito picks up viruses when it feeds on an animal that's been infected. The virus reproduces inside the mosquito, and then gets passed on when the mosquito bites another host to feed on its blood.

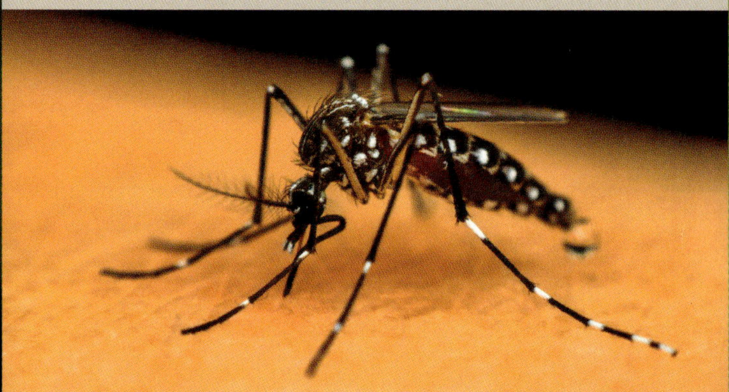

Female mosquitoes find a mammal host to feed on by sniffing out chemicals that it gives off, such as the carbon dioxide in its breath.

The yellow fever mosquito has black and white markings on its legs. Scientists think this is used as identification for mating, as well as being a form of camouflage.

AFRICAN PRAYING MANTIS

The African praying mantis, sometimes also known as the African lined mantis, relies on its sense of sight to find food, so is active during the day. It lives in the wild in many wooded regions south of the Sahara Desert. However, its large size and fascinating hunting behavior has made it a popular pet, and it is kept by people all over the world.

FACT FILE

- **Scientific name:** *Sphodromantis lineola*
- **Class:** insect
- **Length:** up to 3.1 in (8 cm)
- **Home:** wooded areas in Central and Southern Africa
- **Diet:** other arthropods

SKILLFUL CATCH

Praying mantises get their name because the way they stand upright with their forelegs folded makes it look like they are praying. However, "preying mantis" would be just as fitting a name, because these insects are predators! They stay very still, blending into the background and waiting for prey to come along. Then they reach out with their strong, spiked forelegs to grab it. They eat whatever they can catch, and females sometimes eat the males after mating.

This African praying mantis is holding a cockroach firmly in its forelegs while it settles in for a meal.

SUPER SENSES

Many praying mantis species have excellent vision, and the African praying mantis is no exception. Their large compound eyes are made up of thousands of smaller components. Those at the edges of the eye are especially good at spotting motion. When a mantis sees something moving, it will swivel its head to get a better look with the central part of its eye. They also use their antennae to detect movement and to recognize the scent of food or a mate.

This praying mantis is cleaning itself. Removing debris keeps the mantis moving efficiently and its sensory organs working well.

African praying mantises are usually green to blend in with their surroundings, but they can also be brown or brownish-green.

DEATHSTALKER SCORPION

All scorpions sting, but the venom of some is stronger than that of others. The deathstalker scorpion gets its name because of its powerful venom, which can sometimes be strong enough to kill a human. However, they only attack humans and large animals when threatened, and spend their time looking for much smaller prey, such as spiders and centipedes.

FACT FILE

- **Scientific name:** *Leiurus quinquestriatus*
- **Class:** arachnid
- **Length:** up to 4.3 in (11 cm)
- **Home:** desert regions of North Africa and the Middle East
- **Diet:** arthropods and other invertebrates

DESERT DWELLERS

Deathstalker scorpions live in deserts where it is both very hot and very dry. They avoid the worst of the heat by sheltering in burrows during the day. They sometimes dig their own burrows, but they also take over the abandoned burrows of other animals. Deathstalker scorpions get much of the water they need from the bodies of their prey, although they do drink sometimes.

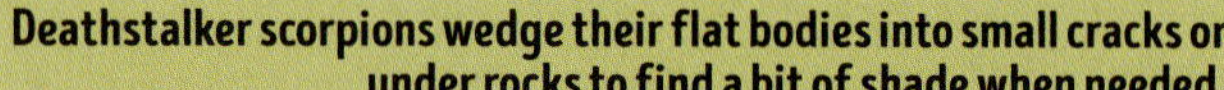

Deathstalker scorpions wedge their flat bodies into small cracks or under rocks to find a bit of shade when needed.

USEFUL VENOM?

Deathstalker venom paralyzes a prey animal, making it easier for the scorpion to eat. The venom contains a mix of chemicals that act on the victim's nerves. Scientists have been able to test several of the different chemicals that the venom contains. They have found that one chemical attaches itself to cancer cells, but not healthy cells, helping to pinpoint their location. This has paved the way for a new, harmless treatment that helps doctors to find and extract cancerous tissue in the human body.

This side view shows the deathstalker's stinger at the end of its tail, which is used to deliver powerful venom to its prey.

The deathstalker scorpion lives in dry desert regions. Its exoskeleton has a waxy coating which stops its body from losing too much water in the heat.

GIANT AFRICAN MILLIPEDE

In the world of bugs, the giant African millipede is a true whopper! There are about 10,000 species of millipede living on Earth today, and this is the largest one, reaching lengths of up to 12 inches (30 cm). Yet even this giant millipede would have been dwarfed by one of its prehistoric ancestors: *Arthropleura*, an 8.5-ft (2.6-m) long monster that lived about 300 million years ago.

FACT FILE

- **Scientific name:** *Archispirostreptus gigas*
- **Class:** myriapod
- **Length:** up to 12 in (30 cm)
- **Home:** tropical rainforests in Africa
- **Diet:** decaying plant matter

NIGHTTIME FEEDERS

These giant millipedes live in the African rainforests. They usually spend the daylight hours curled up safe in burrows in the soil or in rotting wood, then come out at night to feed on leaf litter and other decaying organic matter. This food is rich in nutrients, and anything that the millipede's body doesn't need is excreted to form a layer of new soil on the forest floor.

Despite reaching the size of a 12-inch (30-cm) ruler, giant millipedes only have around 300 legs—far fewer legs than *Eumillipes persephone* (see page 152).

GOOD DEFENCE

Millipedes are at risk from predators, such as birds, reptiles, and small mammals. One strategy they use to stay safe is to coil their body into a tight spiral. With only its back showing, the plates of a millipede's exoskeleton act like body armor. The millipede can also give off a liquid that smells and tastes terrible. It's enough to make a predator think twice about ordering millipede for lunch!

The softer legs and underside of a millipede's body are protected when it curls up into a spiral.

The giant African millipede has poor eyesight and relies on its antennae to smell and feel its way around. Its legs move in a wavelike motion—with each leg lifting a little later than the one behind it.

DESERT LOCUST

Some insects live solitary lives, only meeting up to mate, while others live in vast colonies or swarms. Desert locusts are insects with a bit of an identity crisis—they often live a solitary lifestyle, but when the conditions are right they develop a different body form and gather into enormous swarms. The swarms descend on grasslands and fields and eat everything in sight. These events, called "plagues," are described in the Bible and other ancient writings.

FACT FILE

- **Scientific name:** *Schistocerca gregaria*
- **Class:** insect
- **Length:** up to 3.5 in (9 cm)
- **Home:** grasslands and deserts of Africa and Southwest Asia
- **Diet:** plants

GRASSHOPPER OR LOCUST?

Locusts are basically grasshoppers. The only scientific difference between locusts and grasshoppers is that locusts can sometimes form swarms when the conditions are right—this is called becoming "gregarious." Many grasshopper species never do this, and even locusts only do it some of the time. When they are not swarming, they live a regular grasshopper lifestyle, munching on grass and causing little fuss.

When a desert locust is in its solitary phase, its body is mainly green or tan. Its color changes when it becomes gregarious and attracted to other locusts.

These desert locusts are feasting on cabbage. Swarms can decimate agricultural land as the locusts eat all the vegetation they can find —leaves, shoots, flowers, fruit, seeds, stems, and even bark.

SIGNAL TO CHANGE

In dry periods, desert locusts are forced to crowd into the last remaining areas of plants. As they look for a meal, their bodies rub up against each other, and this triggers the release of a hormone into their brain. The hormone changes their appearance as well as their behavior. The locusts' bodies become stronger and they change color. They are now attracted to other locusts, and they gather in huge swarms.

The change from solitary to gregarious can take place as a nymph, shown here, or as an adult. A gregarious nymph can also molt into a gregarious adult.

WORLD TRAVELERS

Desert locusts only get their wings when the nymphs take their adult form. Once this happens, vast swarms can take off in search of new food sources. These swarms can be made up of billions of individual locusts. They travel at the speed of the wind, and can cover more than 100 miles (160 km) a day. In 1988, one swarm crossed the Atlantic Ocean from Africa to the Caribbean in just 10 days!

It doesn't take long for a swarm of desert locusts to fill the sky, as shown here in Kenya.

CROP IMPACT

Wherever a locust swarm lands, the locusts feed, and these hungry insects can quickly strip a farmer's field. Each individual locust can eat up to its own body weight in plants each day. That might not sound like a lot, but when multiplied by the huge number of locusts in a swarm, it really adds up! Plagues of locusts can destroy food supplies over a large area, leading to shortages and even famine.

MADAGASCAN HISSING COCKROACH

One of the world's largest species of cockroach can be found on the island of Madagascar. When they produce a hissing sound, it makes them even scarier! Yet these cockroaches are nothing to be afraid of. They eat leaf litter on the rainforest floor and play an important role in preserving their environment by recycling nutrients into the soil.

FACT FILE

- **Scientific name:** *Gromphadorhina portentosa*
- **Class:** insect
- **Length:** up to 4 in (10 cm)
- **Home:** rainforests in Madagascar
- **Diet:** decaying plant matter

SPECIAL EGG CASE

After mating, female cockroaches of this species do not lay eggs on the ground. Instead, the eggs are protected inside a long, yellow egg case called an ootheca. Most cockroach species deposit the ootheca on the ground, but a female Madagascan hissing cockroach carries it inside her body. It is here that the eggs hatch, and then the nymphs emerge from the mother's body. It looks like she is giving birth to live young.

Female cockroaches sometimes push the ootheca part of the way out of their body to allow air to dry the egg sac.

With its poor eyesight, the Madagascan hissing cockroach relies on its antennae to navigate its surroundings, and its spiny legs offer a good grip on tree bark or rough terrain.

MAKING NOISE

Madagascan hissing cockroaches are famous for the noises they make. The noise is produced by forcing air through small tubes called spiracles that the cockroaches use for breathing. Males will hiss to find a female and then hiss in a slightly different way to woo her once they get close. Males also hiss when fighting other males. The cockroaches also hiss to frighten predators into thinking that they are a snake!

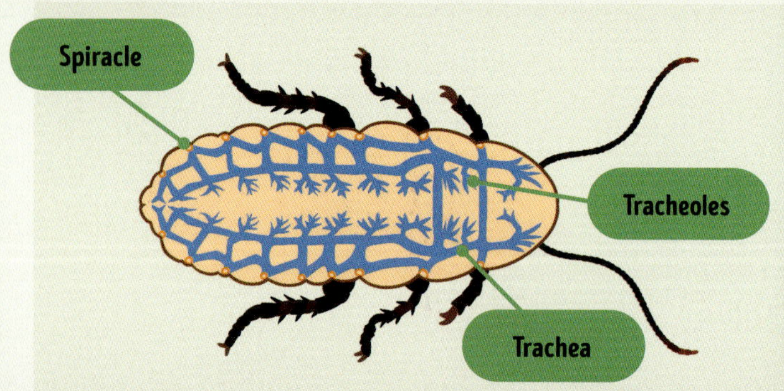

This artwork shows the cockroach's inner breathing tubes and spiracles. The cockroach uses these tubes to make different hissing sounds.

TAILLESS WHIP SCORPION

This odd-looking creature has "scorpion" in its name, but it's not a scorpion. It looks a bit like a spider, but it's not a spider either! It's a different kind of arachnid called an amblypygid, sometimes also known as a whip spider or tailless whip scorpion. There are a few hundred species of amblypygid living in warm tropical areas around the world. This one is found in Kenya and Tanzania.

FACT FILE

- **Scientific name:** *Damon diadema*
- **Class:** arachnid
- **Length:** body up to 2 in (5 cm); leg span up to 21.7 in (55 cm)
- **Home:** caves or tree trunks in East Africa
- **Diet:** other arthropods

Tailless whip scorpions like to live in caves, under rocks, or in dark, damp places.

UNUSUAL BODIES

Tailless whip scorpions are arachnids, so they have eight legs. However, the front pair of legs is much longer and thinner than the others. The animal runs or walks on its other six legs, and uses the front ones more like antennae, feeling for tiny vibrations made by potential prey. Once the tailless whip scorpion senses prey nearby, it uses the set of long, armlike pedipalps at the front of its body to reach out and grab it.

A tailless whip scorpion's pedipalps end in sharp claws which help it to hold prey as it eats.

PIGGY BACK

A female tailless whip scorpion lays eggs, then attaches them to the underside of her abdomen using a thin membrane. This way she can carry them around with her and keep them safe until they hatch. Once the nymphs emerge from their eggs, they climb onto her back. As they grow, they shed their skin. Unlike many insects, there is no fixed number of molts for a tailless whip scorpion. They will continue to grow and molt throughout their life. In the males, larger pedipalps show when they've reached adulthood.

This female is carrying her young. The nymphs' bodies are pale, but will darken as they get older.

ASIA

Asia is the world's largest continent, in terms of both population and land area. It has a huge range of different environments, including the world's tallest mountains and several of the planet's largest deserts. There are also vast grasslands and steamy tropical forests, as well as large areas of frozen tundra in the far north. Asia really does have it all—and that includes some of the world's most fascinating bugs!

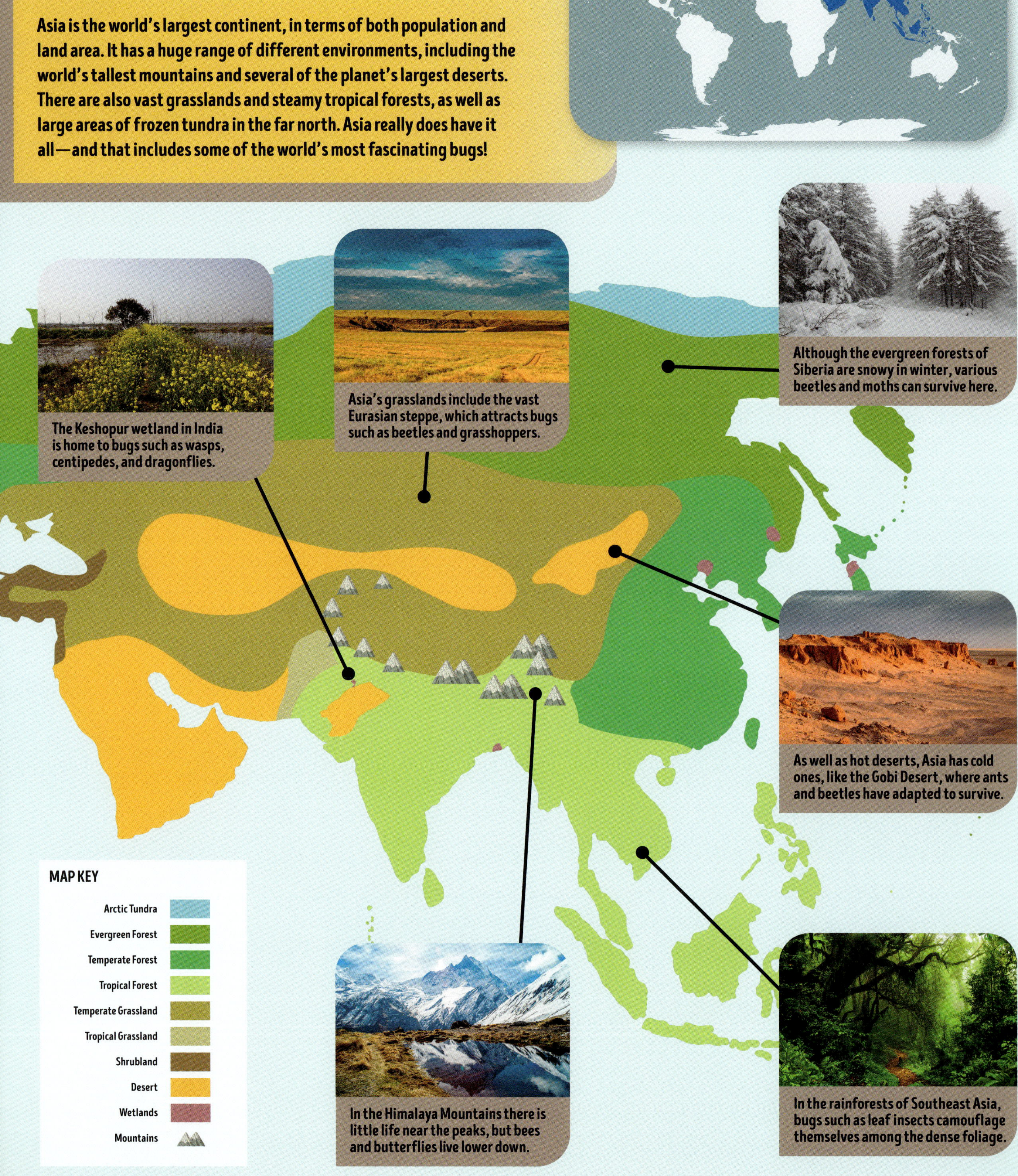

VIOLIN BEETLE

Some insects make chirping, buzzing, or humming noises by rubbing parts of their body against each other, like a violinist rubs a bow over the strings of their instrument. However, these long-necked beetles from Southeast Asia are different. They may have bodies that look a bit like violins, but you won't find them in a symphony orchestra —they don't really make any noise at all!

FACT FILE

- **Scientific name:** *Mormolyce phyllodes*
- **Class:** insect
- **Length:** up to 4 in (10 cm)
- **Home:** tropical rainforests of Southeast Asia
- **Diet:** insect larvae

FUNGUS LOVERS

The warm, damp conditions in the rainforest are perfect for fungi. Types of a fungus known as bracket fungus (or shelf fungus) grow straight out from the trunks of trees, and this is where young violin beetles make their home. The larvae live between the layers of bracket fungi, feeding on insect larvae. After about eight to nine months, they pupate in the fungus, and eventually the adult beetle crawls out of a tiny hole to the outside world.

Bracket fungi grow on the trunks of trees in the rainforest. They get all the nutrients they need from the wood.

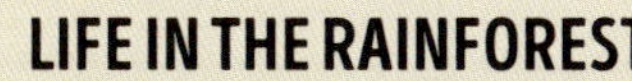

LIFE IN THE RAINFOREST

Adult violin beetles emerge in late summer and live for a few months before the colder weather sets in. They crawl and fly through the rainforest, looking for insect larvae to eat. They have an unusually long neck, with their eyes and antennae at the tip of the head. When threatened, the beetles can squirt a foul-smelling liquid from their abdomen. The smell alone is enough to deter most predators, but the acid can also burn their eyes and skin.

A violin beetle's wafer-thin body allows it to hide in cracks and crevices and under leaves or tree bark.

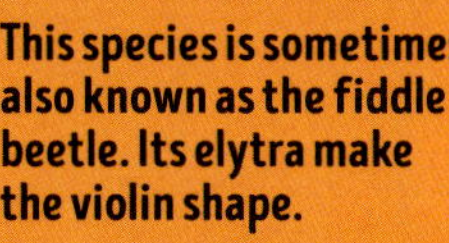

This species is sometimes also known as the fiddle beetle. Its elytra make the violin shape.

GIANT MALAYSIAN LEAF INSECT

Predators eat meat, so when they're looking for a tasty meal they'll pass straight over anything that looks like a plant. If you're an animal and want to avoid becoming that meal, then a good way to do that is to resemble vegetation as closely as possible! That's the strategy of the giant Malaysian leaf insect. It looks so much like a leaf that predators—and even people—are often fooled.

FACT FILE

- **Scientific name:** *Pulchriphyllium giganteum*
- **Class:** insect
- **Length:** up to 4.5 in (11.5 cm)
- **Home:** tropical rainforests of Southeast Asia
- **Diet:** leaves

Although it takes its name from Malaysia, this species is also found in Indonesia and Thailand. Here you can see the leaflike parts of its body.

SURVIVING IN THE FOREST

Female leaf insects stay motionless on a tree when laying eggs, and let the eggs just fall to the ground. The eggs are camouflaged too, and look like tiny brown seeds or insect poop. The nymphs that hatch out look like small adults, but they are brown to match the dead leaves on the rainforest floor. As they grow, they will gradually turn green and make their way into the trees, where their new color will blend in.

Leaf insects often spend their entire adult life on the same tree. This nymph will soon turn green to match its surroundings.

MASTERS OF CAMOUFLAGE

The Malaysian giant leaf insect disguises itself as the leaves that it eats—truly a case of "you are what you eat!" Its leaf camouflage is incredibly detailed. Its body is shaped like a large leaf, and its legs look like smaller pieces of leaf. It even has structures that look like a leaf's veins, and brown spots on the edges which make it look like the leaf is damaged or drying out.

A leaf insect completes the resemblance to a leaf by staying as still as possible, just like a real leaf would.

TRAPDOOR SPIDER

Imagine you're an insect, just minding your own business on the rainforest floor in Southeast Asia. You're crawling along, looking for something to eat, when you trip over a thin thread of silk. Before you know it, a spider has appeared from nowhere, bursting out of a hidden burrow like a fanged, hungry jack-in-the-box. You've just become a meal for a trapdoor spider!

FACT FILE

- **Scientific name:** genus *Liphistius* (many species)
- **Class:** arachnid
- **Length:** body up to 1.4 in (3.6 cm) depending on species
- **Home:** tropical rainforests of Southeast Asia
- **Diet:** other arthropods

BUILDING A TRAP

Liphistius spiders dig a burrow in the soil and spin silken threads to line it, which extend outside as tripwires. They spin a flap to cover the entrance, and use soil and moss to camouflage it against the surrounding ground. The spider hides inside, just under the trapdoor. Trapdoor spiders only leap out when something touches a tripwire. Even then, the spider keeps its hindmost two legs inside the burrow.

Most *Liphistius* traps have 6–8 silk tripwires radiating out from the burrow.

CAVE DWELLERS

Some *Liphistius* species make their home in rainforest caves, building nests on the floor or wall of the cave. These nests still have the same kind of tripwires, but they also have a back door as a kind of escape route. If the spider pops out and discovers that a predator has touched a tripwire, they can quickly retreat back into their nest and escape through this back door.

This trapdoor spider has built its nest in the gaps and crevices of a cave, to await unsuspecting prey that passes by.

Trapdoor spiders tend to stay in their burrows which are lined with silk. Males only leave their burrows when they're looking for a female mate.

INDIAN STICK INSECT

Stick insects go by lots of different names: stick bugs, walking sticks, even ghost insects! There are many species around the world, and they are all masters of camouflage with bodies that look like twigs. Even their thin, spindly legs look like smaller twigs. One species, which comes from Tamil Nadu in India, has become a popular pet and is often kept in school classrooms.

FACT FILE

- **Scientific name:** *Carausius morosus*
- **Class:** insect
- **Length:** body up to 4 in (10 cm)
- **Home:** tropical rainforests
- **Diet:** leaves

SINGLE PARENTS

Male stick insects are rare, but luckily the females don't necessarily need to find one to breed. Stick insects can reproduce by laying eggs that haven't been fertilized by a male. The nymphs that hatch from these eggs are nearly always female, and look like small clones of their mother. Male nymphs are usually produced only when a male and a female insect mate. The nymphs molt several times as they grow.

These are the eggs of a female stick insect—they look like tiny pots with lids! A female can lay around seven eggs per day.

A stick insect has a hard exoskeleton that looks just like wood. It uses its antennae to sense its surroundings, and special sticky pads on its feet help it to cling to the vertical surface of this tree trunk.

KEEPING HIDDEN

Stick insects use their excellent camouflage to help avoid predators. They look so much like sticks or twigs that when they stay still, they can be very hard to spot. They are nocturnal, staying hidden during the day and only coming out to feed at night. If caught by a predator, they can shed a leg to escape. The next time the stick insect molts, it will regrow the missing limb.

Even with a contrasting color, it's not always easy to spot a stick insect among rainforest twigs and foliage.

PLAYING DEAD

Predators, such as birds, lizards, and spiders, will all eat stick insects if they get a chance. If a stick insect's camouflage doesn't succeed in keeping it hidden, it has another line of defense. The insect can drop to the ground and play dead, remaining completely still for hours on end. A predator that is only interested in live prey will lose interest and move on. Predators with vision are better at seeing objects in motion.

This stick insect has dropped to the ground to play dead. It will stay rigid and motionless for several hours if necessary.

POPULAR PETS

Stick insects are harmless to humans, and their unusual bodies are fascinating to watch, so they are often kept as pets. Some people raise them from eggs, watching them go through all the different stages of their life cycle. However, they must be handled very gently—or even better, not handled at all. Rough handling might make them lose a leg!

Stick insects are delicate creatures but they are calm and easy to care for.

RED SPIDER MITE

Also known as the two-spotted spider mite, the red spider mite is a species of mite that feeds on plants. Although it is native to Asia and Europe, it has spread and now appears as a pest in yards and gardens in many parts of the world. It gets its name from its red color and its habit of spinning silken webbing like that of a spider. These mites often cluster in large colonies on the host plants that they eat.

FACT FILE

- **Scientific name:** *Tetranychus urticae*
- **Class:** arachnid
- **Length:** about 0.02 in (0.4 mm)
- **Home:** temperate regions
- **Diet:** plant sap

REPRODUCING

Female red spider mites can lay eggs without needing a male to fertilize them, but these eggs will all develop into males. Fertilized eggs can develop into either males or females. Six-legged larvae hatch from the eggs, and this stage is followed by two eight-legged nymph stages. Finally, the mites take their adult form. During colder months they are red, but at other times of year they look greenish-yellow, with two dark spots.

A hand lens when you're out and about can be useful to see bugs in more detail. Even as adults, red spider mites are extremely small.

PEST CONTROL

Red spider mites suck the sap from plants, which can weaken and sometimes even kill them. This makes the mites a pest for farmers and gardeners. The mites prefer warm, dry conditions, so keeping plants wet stops them from reproducing. In some places, people bring in another mite species that preys on red spider mites. These predators don't feed on plants, only on the spider mites and their eggs.

In this red spider mite infestation on a leaf, you can see eggs as well as adults, and light patches where the leaf has been eaten.

This red spider mite colony has hundreds of individuals (see below). The mites have spun a web as a protective covering over the plants that they eat.

SILKWORM MOTH

Humans have domesticated many large animals, such as cows and pigs. But did you know that we've also domesticated insects? The silkworm moth lives in China and other parts of Asia. For thousands of years, people there have been making fabric from the silk that these caterpillars spin for their cocoons. They have been carefully bred from a wild ancestor, so that today these moths can only survive on silk farms.

FACT FILE

- **Scientific name:** *Bombyx mori*
- **Class:** insect
- **Length:** caterpillars up to 2 in (5 cm); adults' wingspan up to 1.6 in (4 cm)
- **Home:** lives in captivity (wild ancestors lived in wooded areas)
- **Diet:** mulberry leaves

MAKING SILK

Silkworm moths lay their eggs on the leaves of a mulberry tree and, once they hatch, the caterpillars eat the leaves. After about six weeks of eating, growing, and molting, the caterpillars spin fine strands of silk to form a delicate cocoon. To make silk cloth, people put the cocoons in hot water to separate the strands. This process kills the pupa inside, and people often eat them. The silk is then spun into fine cloth.

If this silkworm cocoon on a mulberry leaf was unraveled and stretched out, it would be more than 0.6 mile (1 km) long!

A CHANGING SPECIES

Over centuries of domestication, the silkworm moth has evolved. It has become used to living in crowded conditions, and it now spins a bigger cocoon. The adult moths can no longer fly, and they have lost the coloration that camouflaged them in the wild. Animal rights groups are campaigning for people to use discarded cocoons to make silk, instead of killing the pupae. The difficulty is that instead of a single thread of silk, the silk in a discarded cocoon has been cut many times.

Silkworm moth caterpillars have evolved to grow faster and get bigger than their wild ancestors ever did.

The silkworm moth has been bred in captivity and can no longer fly, because its wings are too small to carry the weight of its body.

GOLDEN-SPOTTED TIGER BEETLE

This insect belongs to a group of beetles known as ground beetles. Although they can fly short distances, ground beetles prefer to race quickly along the ground. The tiger beetle —of which there are several species—gets its name from its aggressive predatory behavior. Golden-spotted tiger beetles can be found in sandy areas throughout Southeast Asia, such as sand dunes, shorelines, mangroves, and forests.

FACT FILE

- **Scientific name:** *Cicindela aurulenta*
- **Class:** insect
- **Length:** up to 0.7 in (1.8 cm)
- **Home:** sandy areas near shorelines in Southeast Asia
- **Diet:** arthropods and other small animals

PREDATORY BEHAVIOR

Golden-spotted tiger beetles are predators, both as larvae and as adults. The larvae live in underground burrows, waiting near the burrow entrance for prey animals to wander close enough to catch. Hooks on their abdomen keep the beetles anchored to their burrow so struggling prey don't pull them out. As adults, they chase after prey on their long, thin legs. Tiger beetles are impressively fast runners, covering more than 100 times their body length per second!

This artwork shows tiger beetle larvae in their underground burrows. They use their flat head to seal the opening, and will lunge at any prey that passes by.

A tiger beetle's elytra have six large spots, with two smaller spots on the shoulders. These colors help the tiger beetles to identify each other as members of the same species.

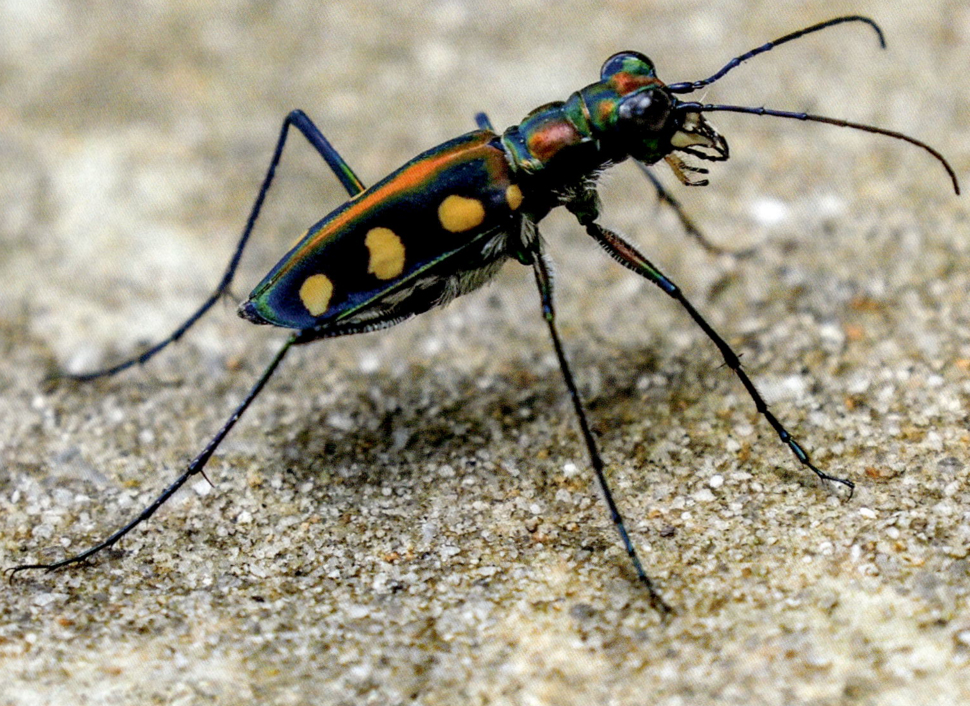

STOP AND GO

There may be a downside to being so fast. Sometimes, when speeding after prey, a tiger beetle will suddenly stop for a moment before resuming the chase. Scientists think this is because the beetles are moving so quickly, their eyes can't gather enough light to focus on their prey. So the beetle must briefly pause to reorient itself before continuing the hunt. This is known as a stop-and-go chase pattern.

Golden-spotted tiger beetles have large, bulging eyes that give them a wide field of vision to find and track their prey.

WATER FLEA

Despite its name, the water flea is not related to the fleas that live on pet cats and dogs. In fact, it's not even an insect! It's a type of tiny crustacean, meaning that it's more closely related to woodlice and lobsters than it is to beetles or ants. It gets its name because its body shape is a little bit flealike, and it swims in a jerky motion that resembles the movement of a jumping flea.

FACT FILE

- **Scientific name:** *Daphnia pulex*
- **Class:** crustacean
- **Length:** up to 0.1 in (3 mm)
- **Home:** freshwater
- **Diet:** bacteria and algae

The outer part of a water flea's body is transparent. This keeps it camouflaged in its surroundings and allows you to see the organs inside.

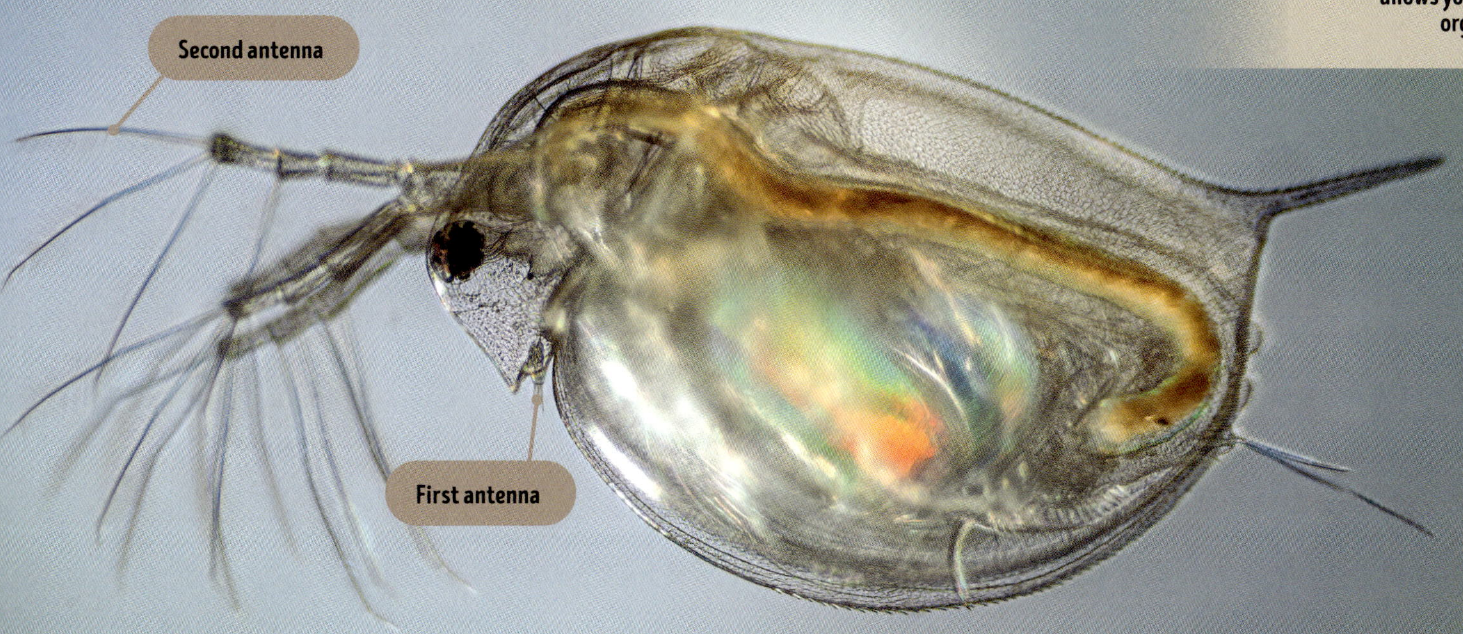

PRODUCING YOUNG

Water fleas can produce young in two ways. They can use sexual reproduction, where a male and female mate—this mainly happens in the winter, or at other times when less food is available. The young produced this way will be a mix of males and females. However, in the summer, the female produces eggs without needing a male to fertilize them. This process is called parthenogenesis, and the eggs will all hatch into females.

A female water flea carries eggs inside her body, giving them time to develop before they are released the next time she molts.

POND LIFE

Water fleas mainly live in lakes and ponds, including Lake Fukami-ike in Japan, where scientists have studied their life cycle. To eat, water fleas force water through their bodies and filter out anything good, such as algae, bacteria, or decaying plant matter. They prefer still water, because they're not strong enough to swim in a current. The fleas have an extra set of antennae (shown above), which they beat to propel them through the water. This gives their swimming a jerky, hopping style, like a jumping flea on land. They swim deeper during the day to avoid predators, then come up nearer the surface at night to feed.

Water fleas make a tasty meal for larger pond animals, such as newts.

ASIAN GIANT HORNET

Hornets are large wasps that form colonies, and the Asian giant hornet is the largest species of hornet in the world. Also known as the Japanese giant hornet, this fierce predator with a powerful sting lives in forests throughout many parts of Asia. In recent years, international trade has seen it spread accidentally into North America and Europe, but authorities there are trying to stop it from spreading any farther.

FACT FILE

- **Scientific name:** *Vespa mandarinia*
- **Class:** insect
- **Length:** queens up to 2 in (5 cm); males and workers up to 1.5 in (3.9 cm)
- **Home:** forested areas
- **Diet:** tree sap and other insects

RAISING YOUNG

Asian giant hornet colonies create nests where they raise their young. Like bees, they build hexagonal cells in these nests where their larvae stay safe as they grow. But unlike bee larvae, the hornet larvae are carnivorous. The adults catch insects such as bees, then chew their prey up into a smooth paste. Back at the nest, they regurgitate this paste and feed it to the larvae.

Asian giant hornets build their nests in natural crevices (left). The hexagonal cells inside (right) keep the maturing larvae safe (see page 29).

About twice the size of a wasp or honeybee, Asian giant hornets have an orange head, and stripes of dark brown, black, and yellowish-orange on their abdomen.

FIERCE PREDATORS

These huge hornets are predators, attacking other insects in flight using their mandibles—or jaws. They bite them to death and take the bodies back to the nest to feed to the larvae. But the adult worker hornets who hunt for food cannot digest this kind of solid food. Instead, they live off tree sap and the saliva of their larvae, which they exchange while feeding them. Although Asian giant hornet colonies sometimes attack each other, no other insect species will take them on. The only known predator is a bird called the honey buzzard.

Asian giant hornets will fight each other to defend their nest, using their stingers and clawlike mandibles.

RAIDING PARTIES

Unlike many other wasp species, Asian giant hornets actively attack the nests of bees and other wasp species. At first, solitary worker hornets wait near a nest entrance to catch prey. Then they signal to other hornets to join them, by releasing a chemical scent from a gland near their stinger. Soon up to 50 hornets will attack a nest together. In the space of just a few hours, they can kill more than 20,000 bees! Then they eat the pupae and larvae living inside the nest. This makes them a pest for farmers, who rely on the honeybees to pollinate their crops.

Asian giant hornets use their large compound eyes to spot food and their mandibles are strong enough to decapitate their prey.

FIGHTING BACK

Asian giant hornets often prey on the nests of the Japanese honeybee, but these bees have found a way to fight back. If a hornet comes, they detect the scent the hornet leaves to mark the nest, and send more bee defenders to protect the entrance. Hundreds of bees surround the hornet, vibrating their wing muscles, which generates heat and increases levels of carbon dioxide. The bees can withstand these conditions, but it soon kills the hornet. Once it's dead, it can no longer report back to its nest mates and tell them where the bees' nest is.

These Japanese honeybees have created a defensive "bee ball" that can reach temperatures of up to 115 °F (46 °C), killing the attacking hornet.

JEWEL BEETLE

This is one insect that really lives up to its name! Jewel beetles have such beautiful iridescent elytra (hard forewings) that they're sometimes collected and made into jewelery. This traditional craft is popular in Southeast Asia, where craftspeople also attach beetle wings to paintings and fabric. There are many different species known as "jewel beetles"—this one is found in Japan.

FACT FILE

- **Scientific name:** *Chrysochroa fulgidissima*
- **Class:** insect
- **Length:** up to 1.6 in (4 cm)
- **Home:** woodlands in Japan
- **Diet:** wood and other plant matter

WOOD BORERS

Jewel beetles are part of a larger group of beetles known as wood-boring beetles. This is because the larvae bore through plants, such as trees and shrubs, while feeding. They often prefer rotting wood, and they dig into the roots, trunks, stems, and branches. Because they tend to eat rotting wood rather than green shoots, the beetles help the natural decomposition of their surroundings.

Jewel beetle larvae have a tiny head that's sunken into a wide, flattened thorax. They are often known as "flat-headed borers."

FOREST JEWELS

Like many other insects with shimmering metallic colors, the colors of the jewel beetle are not caused by pigment in its body. Instead, they're the result of microscopic structures within the cuticle—the tough, flexible outer body covering. These tiny structures reflect light in a certain way that gives the beetle its metallic sheen. Although these structures are much too small to see with the naked eye, scientists have used powerful microscopes to investigate them.

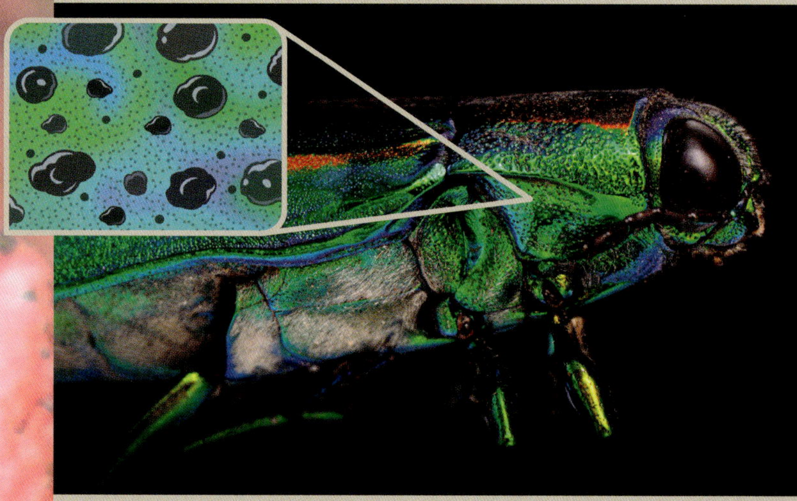

Although you can see dimples on the surface of this jewel beetle, even smaller microscopic dimples are what cause the color fluctuations.

Potential mates easily recognize the jewel beetle's long, slender body and bright metallic sheen, which shows the colors of the rainbow when viewed from different angles.

SAPPHIRE TARANTULA

When you think of a spider, you probably picture something black or brown. Chances are, your mental image is not bright blue! But this rare spider, found in southeastern India, is known as the sapphire spider because of its stunning color. It's often also called the peacock tarantula or the Gooty sapphire, after the Indian town where it was first found and described in 1899.

FACT FILE

- **Scientific name:** *Poecilotheria metallica*
- **Class:** arachnid
- **Length:** body up to 2.4 in (6 cm); leg span up to 7.9 in (20 cm)
- **Home:** forested areas
- **Diet:** crickets, moths, and grasshoppers

Sapphire tarantulas live in tree hollows and bark crevices in dense, humid forests. They are fast movers, especially if they are startled by a bright light.

CHANGING COLOR

Young sapphire tarantulas are much less blue, but their color gradually brightens as they get older. These spiders live in hollows in the trunks of tall trees, which they line with silk. Their eyes are very sensitive to light and they hunt by sight. They can also run fast if startled, and bite if threatened, though their venom is not deadly to humans. However, with fangs that can grow to nearly 0.8 inch (2 cm) long, their bite can still be very painful!

These blue hairs don't irritate, like they do with some tarantulas (see page 55), but the venomous fangs can give a nasty bite.

CRITICAL CONDITION

There were no recorded sightings of the sapphire tarantula for over 100 years, until it was spotted again in 2001 in a different region from where it was first found. Scientists now think the original specimen from 1899, which was discovered in a rail yard, may have arrived there by train. The spider's true habitat is a fairly small region of forest that is being destroyed by logging and clearing land for farming. As a result of this habitat loss, the spider is classified as critically endangered.

Although the tarantulas are endangered in the wild, many people around the world keep them as pets.

ORCHID MANTIS

Beautiful orchid flowers grow in the tropical rainforests of Southeast Asia. They attract insects, such as flies and wasps, who visit to feed on nectar and end up carrying away pollen when they leave. However, for some insects, the orchid marks the end of their journey. That's because they get gobbled up by a cleverly camouflaged orchid mantis!

FACT FILE

- **Scientific name:** *Hymenopus coronatus*
- **Class:** insect
- **Length:** males up to 1 in (2.5 cm); females up to 2.4 in (6 cm)
- **Home:** tropical rainforests
- **Diet:** other insects

FLOWER MIMICS

The orchid mantis is a species of praying mantis. Most species in this group are green, brown, or black, which helps them to blend in with leaves and stems. Orchid mantises take a different approach. Their bodies are delicate shades of pink and white, just like the orchid flowers where they live. An orchid mantis can change its color from pink to brown to match its background, so when a flower dies and its petals begin to turn brown, the orchid mantis can look a little brown too (see male mantis on page 127).

This orchid mantis is well camouflaged against a flower stem—it's difficult to tell at a glance which part is flower and which part is insect.

BIG AND SMALL

The nymphs that hatch from eggs have the same basic body shape as their parents, but they are dark orange with black legs and a black head. This makes them resemble other bugs that taste bad, which puts predators off. They continue to grow and go through multiple moults. Males only grow to about half the size of the females, and they don't live as long either—only about six months, compared to a female's life of about eight months.

Young orchid mantis nymphs are a garish color. After their first moult, they develop more delicate pink and white shades.

The orchid mantis has evolved to look like a flower, with petal-shaped legs and delicate coloring.

SAFETY TACTICS

An orchid mantis's colors do more than just help it to catch prey—they also help to keep it safe! Animals such as birds, bats, frogs, and lizards all eat orchid mantises, but they often have trouble spotting them among the flowers. However, the male mantises are not safe from their own kind! The females are much larger and often eat their partner after mating.

A male orchid mantis (left) is risking his life when he approaches a larger female (right) to mate.

HIDDEN THREAT

Orchid mantises are ambush predators, meaning that they hide and wait for prey to come to them. Their flower camouflage is a great help with this! An orchid mantis climbs a plant until it reaches a cluster of flowers. Then it holds on with its four hind legs and sways from side to side, like a flower being blown by a breeze. Once an insect approaches, it quickly grabs it with its front legs and begins to eat.

The front legs of an orchid mantis have a toothed edge that helps with holding on to wriggly prey.

ASIAN BOMBARDIER BEETLE

Some insects, such as the orchid mantis (see page 126), rely on camouflage to stay safe. Others have bright colors to warn predators that they're toxic, or eyespots that make them look like larger animals. But the bombardier beetle's defense mechanism is completely different—and a lot more explosive! They shoot a stream of hot, burning chemicals out of their abdomen.

FACT FILE

- **Scientific name:** *Pheropsophus jessoensis*
- **Class:** insect
- **Length:** up to 0.7 in (1.8 cm)
- **Home:** grasslands and forests in East Asia
- **Diet:** plants and insects

CHEMICAL REACTION

A bombardier beetle's mighty squirt is the result of two different chemicals stored inside its abdomen. The chemicals are kept separate in two sacs. But once they are mixed, they produce a violent chemical reaction. The new chemical they produce is a stinging liquid that can be boiling hot! That's because the chemical reaction produces a lot of heat, very quickly. You can hear a popping sound when a bombardier beetle squirts.

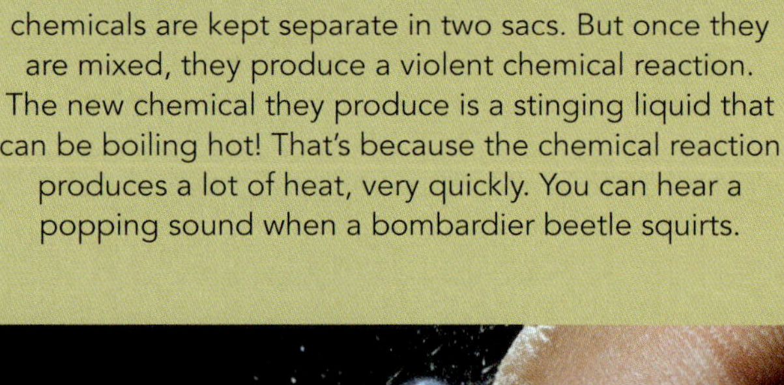

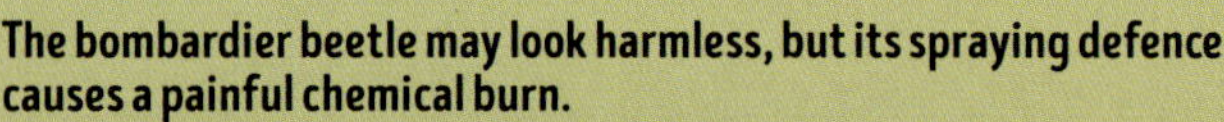

The bombardier beetle may look harmless, but its spraying defence causes a painful chemical burn.

SECOND CHANCE

Some species of toad eat bombardier beetles, and scientists have studied the effects of this. Once a beetle has been eaten, the scientists can hear the sound of a squirt being released inside the toad. Around half the time, the toad would then vomit out the beetle. It might be covered in gooey mucus from the frog's stomach, but the beetle lives to fight another day. The bigger the beetle and the smaller the toad, the more likely it was to be vomited out to safety.

This artwork shows a bombardier beetle that escaped being fully eaten by a Japanese common toad, because its toxic chemicals caused the toad to vomit.

The Asian bombardier beetle is a ground beetle (see page 120), but it will climb into foliage when hunting for food.

MALAYSIAN STALK-EYED FLY

Most sharks have a similar body shape: long and streamlined, like a torpedo. But have you ever seen a hammerhead? Their wide heads, with eyes at the sides, make them look completely different from other sharks. Stalk-eyed flies could be described as the hammerhead sharks of the insect world. Their eyes stick way out to the sides on long eyestalks.

FACT FILE

- **Scientific name:** *Teleopsis dalmanni*
- **Class:** insect
- **Length:** up to 0.3 in (7 mm)
- **Home:** forest streams in Malaysia and other parts of Southeast Asia
- **Diet:** rotting plants

The Malaysian stalk-eyed fly is often found resting on foliage along the banks of freshwater streams, where it feeds and finds a mate.

WEIRD EYES

So why do stalk-eyed flies have such weird-looking eyes? There is a compound eye at the end of each stalk, and having them set so wide apart seems to give the flies a wider field of vision. This may help with spotting potential predators or mates. However, the long eyestalks may make them less aerodynamic when they fly, which would be a disadvantage.

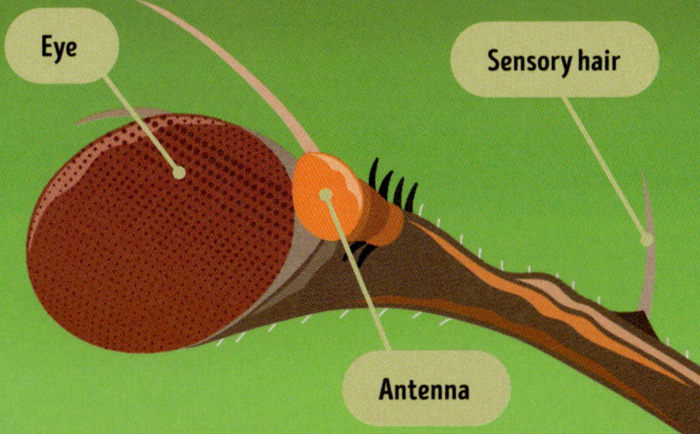

This artwork shows a close-up of the fly's compound eye, which also has sensory hairs and an antenna to detect the environment.

SHOWING OFF

It appears that the main purpose of the long eyestalks is display—in particular, for males to show off to females. A male fly's eyestalks can be wider than its body is long! When choosing a mate, females seem to prefer those males with longer eyestalks. This means that the males with long eyestalks are more likely to mate and pass on their genes, leading to offspring with long eyestalks as well.

The eyestalks of a female fly, shown here, are much smaller than those of the males.

FIREBUG

The word "firebug" is sometimes used for a person who starts fires deliberately. Luckily, the insect known as the firebug gets its name for a completely different reason! These little bugs don't start fires, but their bright red color reminded many people of flames. In fact, the scientific name for the genus comes from Greek words meaning "fire" and "bug."

FACT FILE

- **Scientific name:** *Pyrrhocoris apterus*
- **Class:** insect
- **Length:** up to 0.5 in (1.2 cm)
- **Home:** widespread in temperate regions
- **Diet:** seeds and plant sap

Firebugs are often found in groups and hibernate under tree bark or in other sheltered places. Here, you can see both adults and nymphs—the adults have the big black spots.

DIFFERENT STAGES

Firebugs dig little pits in the ground to lay their eggs, then cover them over. The nymphs that hatch out are red and black, but with a slightly different shape and markings from the adults. They mainly feed on seeds that fall to the ground, particularly from lime trees and mallow plants, or suck plant sap. As they grow, they molt several times over two to three months, and each molt takes them closer to their adult appearance.

Firebugs are part of the "true bugs" grouping (see page 9), with mouthparts for piercing and sucking plant sap, even from a young age like this nymph.

COMING TOGETHER

Firebugs often come together in groups, though they don't form organized colonies in the same way that bees and ants do. Scientists have found that the bugs communicate using chemicals called pheromones. The firebugs can sense, and are attracted to, the pheromones given off by other bugs. Different pheromones serve as a warning when a predator is near. These pheromones are a cue to the bugs to scatter and find safety.

ATLAS BEETLE

The Atlas beetle is a type of rhinoceros beetle like the Hercules beetle from South America (see page 48). Both species are large and fat, with impressive horns, but the Atlas beetle has three horns rather than two. In Greek mythology, Atlas was cursed to bear the weight of the heavens on his shoulders. Like its namesake, the Atlas beetle is also pretty strong!

FACT FILE

- **Scientific name:** *Chalcosoma atlas*
- **Class:** insect
- **Length:** females up to 2.4 in (6 cm); males up to 5.1 in (13 cm)
- **Home:** tropical rainforests of Asia
- **Diet:** larvae eat rotting wood; adults feed on plants and sap

Male Atlas beetles use their impressive horns to fight. The three horns work together to provide extra leverage and strength.

FROM LARVA TO ADULT

Male Atlas beetles have three large horns coming out of their head and thorax, making them look a bit like a miniature version of the dinosaur *Triceratops*. It takes more than a year to reach this adult stage! Larvae live in fallen trees, where they eat the rotting wood, eventually reaching the size of a man's thumb. After pupating, they emerge as adults and feed on sap, fruit, and other plant material.

Females are much smaller than the males, and they do not have the same long horns needed for fighting.

READY TO FIGHT

Atlas beetles have a reputation for being aggressive. The larvae are not predators, but even they will bite if they feel threatened, and their size makes them a formidable opponent. Adult male Atlas beetles often fight with each other when competing to find a mate. They use their horns to try to push their opponent away. Sometimes the battles take place high in a tree, and the loser will fall to the ground.

Atlas beetles use their horns to try to throw their opponent or flip them over, sometimes while balancing on a branch!

ATLAS MOTH

The Atlas beetle is rather large as beetles go (see page 131), so it's no surprise that the Atlas moth is another whopper! This is one of the world's largest lepidopterans—that's the term that entomologists use to refer to both butterflies and moths. The moths rest during the day and become active at night, looking for a mate.

FACT FILE
- **Scientific name:** *Attacus atlas*
- **Class:** insect
- **Length:** body up to 1.6 in (4 cm); wingspan up to 10 in (25 cm)
- **Home:** tropical rainforests
- **Diet:** caterpillars eat leaves; adults do not eat

Like other moths, the Atlas moth tends to rest with its wings spread open.

HUNGRY CATERPILLARS

Female Atlas moths lay their eggs on the leaves of a wide variety of plants, which provide food for the caterpillars once they hatch. The caterpillars are spiky and pale green in color, but each time they molt they take on a slightly darker shade. By the time the caterpillars are ready to pupate, they will have reached a length of up to 4.15 inches (11.5 cm). This usually takes about eight to ten weeks.

Atlas moth caterpillars have waxy, fleshy tubercles (spines) on their back that become larger with each molt.

TIME TO PUPATE

When pupating, the caterpillar spins a silk cocoon for itself. It will stay here for four to six weeks, until it is ready to emerge as an adult moth. The cocoons are woven from silk and leaves, and attached to twigs or branches using the silk. If a bird comes to peck at it, the dangling cocoon will sway back and forth. This makes it harder for the bird's beak to pierce the cocoon and get at the pupa inside.

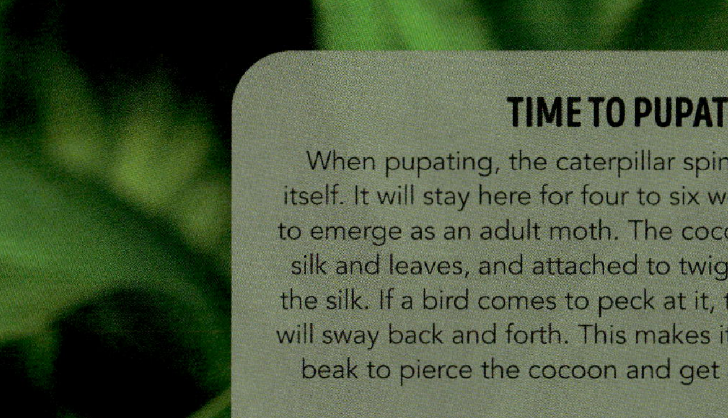

These Atlas caterpillar cocoons are hanging safely from a branch and are cleverly disguised as dead leaves.

RACE AGAINST TIME

Adult Atlas moths do not have mouthparts that allow them to eat. This means they will only live for a few days as adults. Once they have used the stores of fat they built up as larvae, they will die. So it's a race to find a mate before that happens. Females release a special scent, which the males can detect with their antennae. They follow the scent until they find the female.

An Atlas moth's antennae have a feathery, comblike structure, which increases the surface area for collecting scents.

PUTTING OFF PREDATORS

Atlas moth caterpillars use their green color to stay camouflaged and avoid predators. They can also spray chemicals from their abdomen as another line of defense. The adult moths are clumsy fliers, so they tend to come out at night. Their sheer size deters some predators, and they can also play dead if threatened. They sometimes also thrash around on the ground, with the patterns on the tips of their wings giving the appearance of the head of a snake.

Atlas moths are huge! They don't have the largest wingspan (see page 58), but they have the largest wing surface area of any moth.

LANTERNFLY

You'd think that an insect with a name like "lanternfly" would glow, like a firefly does. But this species of insect doesn't produce any light at all! Instead, it gets its name from the long, red structure on its head that looks a bit like a trunk, horn, or long nose. Perhaps people thought it looked like a lantern and believed the myth that it was luminous at night.

FACT FILE

- **Scientific name:** *Pyrops candelaria*
- **Class:** insect
- **Length:** body up to 1.6 in (4 cm)
- **Home:** tropical rainforests
- **Diet:** plant sap

COLORFUL WINGS

The lanternfly's body is usually hidden under its forewings, which it often holds close to the body. They are green with a yellowish-cream veined pattern, marked by some larger spots. Beneath these are the hindwings, which are yellowish-orange with black tips. Lanternflies are part of a group known as planthoppers, and while they do often hop from plant to plant, they can also fly.

This artwork shows the lanternfly's unusually colored wings, which are used for camouflage and to attract a mate.

SAP SUCKERS

In addition to its red "snout," the lanternfly also has a long, thin proboscis. It uses this like a sharp straw, piercing the bark of fruit trees to suck out the sweet sap inside. The bugs are often found on the longan or lychee trees of Southeast Asia, and so are sometimes known as the "longan lanternflies." Nymphs tend to stay on the underside of the lower branches of trees as they feed.

While they feed on tree sap, with their proboscis piercing the bark, lanternflies are at risk from predators, such as birds, lizards, and amphibians.

This insect, with its prominent "nose," is closely related to the alligator bug in South America (see page 52), but it lives in the tropical rainforests of Southeast Asia.

WATER BOATMAN

There are many insect species that spend their lives in water, but not many of them know how to do the backstroke! The water boatman is also known as the "backswimmer" because of the way it lies on its back, just below the surface of the water, and uses its long hind legs to paddle along.

FACT FILE

- **Scientific name:** *Notonecta glauca*
- **Class:** insect
- **Length:** up to 0.6 in (1.6 cm)
- **Home:** freshwater ponds in northern Asia and Europe
- **Diet:** water fleas, small insects, and fish eggs

A water boatman suspends itself just beneath the water's surface as it swims along, upside down, looking for prey.

STAYING UNDERWATER

A water boatman rests under the water's surface, with its front and middle legs, and the back of its abdomen, touching the water's surface. Because the insects are fairly light, the surface tension of the water is enough to keep them from sinking down. They need air to breathe, but they carry a supply with them. Before they go underwater, tiny hairs covering their body trap a thin layer of air. They absorb this air while underwater.

The tiny hairs on a water boatman's legs and abdomen trap air which the bug can absorb, and the hairs keep its body from getting wet.

AMBUSH PREDATOR

Water boatmen are predators that catch and eat a variety of tiny water creatures. They are ambush predators, preferring to sit and wait for prey to come to them. They tend to hide themselves among water plants before reaching out with their front or middle legs to grab prey. They will often feed on mosquito larvae near the water's surface. They also dive deeper to feed on other creatures.

This water boatman has successfully trapped a fly. It takes less energy to hunt near the surface than it does to dive down deeper.

AUSTRALIA AND OCEANIA

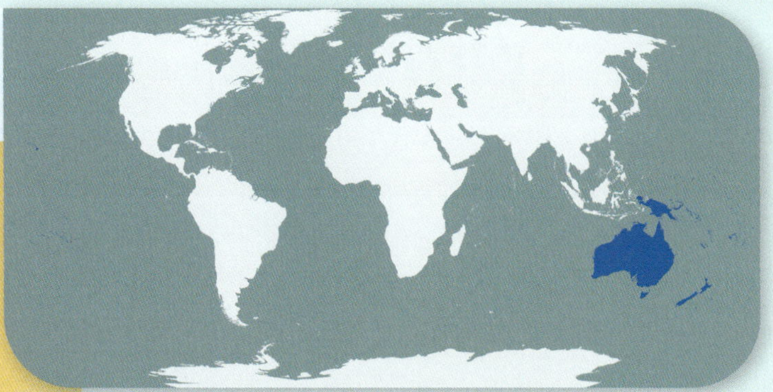

Australia is the smallest of the seven continents, but it is at the heart of a much larger geographic region known as Oceania. This region includes large islands such as New Guinea and New Zealand, as well as many thousands of smaller islands scattered across the south Pacific Ocean. The islands are a mix of low-lying coral atolls and volcanoes rising from the sea floor. This variety provides a range of different environments for bugs and other animals.

New Guinea has one of the largest tropical rainforests in the region, where many spiders and moths thrive.

Some bugs, such as mosquitoes and ants, have adapted to survive in Australia's hot, dry deserts.

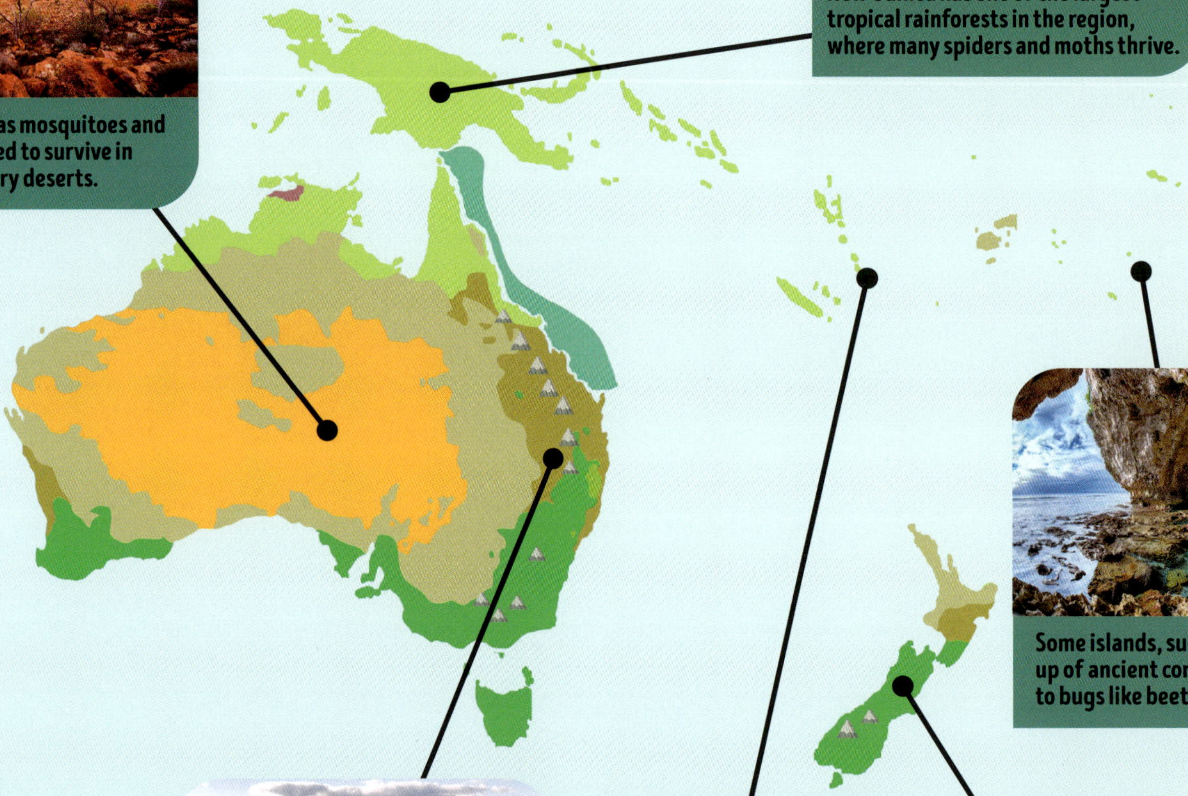

Some islands, such as Niue, are made up of ancient coral reefs, and home to bugs like beetles and butterflies.

Bugs such as wasps and dragonflies can be found in the mountains of the Great Dividing Range.

On the region's many small islands, bugs such as aphids live on the land, while sea skaters live in the water.

In the temperate forests of New Zealand and Australia, bugs such as spiders, beetles, and millipedes thrive.

MAP KEY

- Temperate Forest
- Tropical Forest
- Temperate Grassland
- Tropical Grassland
- Desert
- Wetlands
- Coral Reef
- Mountains

HONEYPOT ANT

Carpenter ants are found all over the world—there are more than 1,500 different species. One species, found only in Australia, is rather special! This ant lives in sandy regions of the continent, where large colonies often build their underground nests at the base of mulga trees. They are often known as "honeypot ants" due to their ingenious way of storing food for the colony.

FACT FILE

- **Scientific name:** *Camponotus inflatus*
- **Class:** insect
- **Length:** worker ants up to 0.3 in (8 mm); repletes up to 0.7 in (1.7 cm)
- **Home:** mainly deserts
- **Diet:** nectar from flowers and honeydew from aphids

These honeypot ants have swollen bodies filled with sweet liquid. Hanging from the ceiling helps their bodies to swell downward with gravity and also keeps them out of the way of the other worker ants.

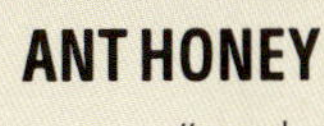

ANT HONEY

Although it's known as "ant honey," the liquid stored by repletes is not quite the same as the honey made by bees—it's runnier and less sweet. The Aboriginal peoples of Australia have harvested these ants for thousands of years. The ant honey is a useful source of sugar, and it's also used to treat sore throats and infections. Recently, scientists have discovered that ant honey contains chemicals that kill some types of bacteria and fungi.

This Aboriginal Australian is digging into a honeypot ant nest to harvest the ants and use their sweet liquid.

THE ROLE OF REPLETES

Like other ant species, a honeypot ant colony is divided up into queens, males, and workers. Many of the workers go out to find food, but about half of them have a different role. These ants are known as "repletes" and their job is to store the sweet liquid that the ants collect for food. Their abdomens can swell to store as much as possible. These ants are like a living larder for the rest of the colony. When needed, they can regurgitate food for other ants to eat.

These repletes are being tended to by other worker ants, who feed them. The repletes never leave the nest.

SMURF BUG

We often give bugs common names that reflect things they resemble, such as the long-necked giraffe weevil (see page 87). One of that insect's weevil relatives gets its common name of "Smurf bug" from its bright blue color. For many people, this bug reminds them of the small, blue humanlike Smurfs from comic books and television. There are many species in the genus *Eupholus*, and they share the same blue color.

FACT FILE

- **Scientific name:** genus *Eupholus* (many species)
- **Class:** insect
- **Length:** up to 1.3 in (3.2 cm), depending on species
- **Home:** tropical islands in New Guinea
- **Diet:** plants

A WORLD OF WEEVILS

Smurf bugs are a type of weevil. These insects are a subgroup of the much larger beetle family. Smurf bugs all share a similar body shape and life cycle. The larvae have no legs when they hatch and often change color with each molt over a period of up to three months, depending on the conditions. Once they pupate and take their adult form, they have elytra (hard forewings), while some species also have hindwings. Both larvae and adults eat plant parts, such as leaves and stems.

Smurf bugs have a long, downward-curving snout and jointed, clublike antennae, used for smelling, feeling, and sensing vibrations.

BRIGHT COLORS

The different species of the genus *Eupholus* are varying shades of blue, and have different patterns. Some have stripes in blue, black, and green, while others have spots. These beetles' rounded bodies are covered in tiny scales and bristles, which can reflect light to give them an iridescent sheen. Their beautiful colors and patterns have made them popular with collectors around the world.

The tiny scales on the body of a Smurf bug can only be seen under a microscope.

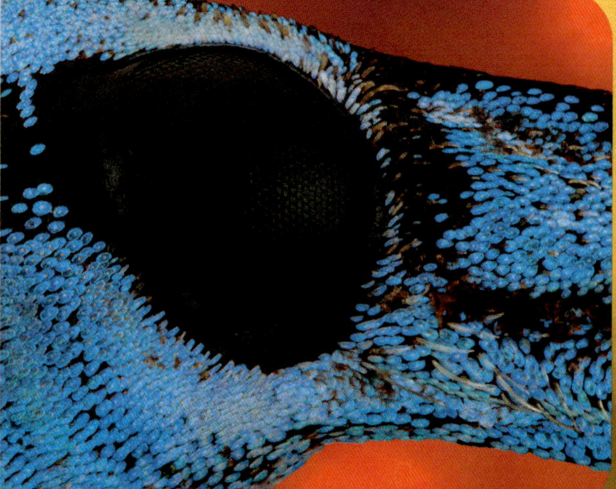

The bright colors of a Smurf bug warn predators to stay away. Many of the species eat yam leaves, which make their bodies toxic.

GIANT WĒTĀ

The giant wētās that live in New Zealand belong to the same insect family as crickets and grasshoppers, but they're super-sized! Although some crickets and grasshoppers have longer bodies, giant wētās are heavier. These nocturnal creatures eat plants, and some species also eat small invertebrates. Their name comes from the language of the indigenous Māori people.

FACT FILE

- **Scientific name:** genus *Deinacrida* (11 species)
- **Class:** insect
- **Length:** up to 2.8 in (7 cm), depending on species
- **Home:** various habitats in New Zealand
- **Diet:** some species only eat plants; others also eat small animals

FINDING A HOME

There are about 100 species of wētā, but most are fairly small. Only the 11 species in the genus *Deinacrida* are known as "giant wētās." The species live in a range of different environments. Some find shelter in the hollow spaces in trees, while others live on the ground. Some giant wētā species are adapted to live high in the mountains.

Giant wētā species that live in trees feed on the leaves and flowers that they produce, as well as lichen and moss.

WĒTĀS UNDER THREAT

Although giant wētās were once common on the main islands of New Zealand, today they are more often found on smaller offshore islands. This is because when people began to colonize the islands in the 1200s, they brought mammals, such as cats, dogs, and rats, which killed the wētās for food. The wētās had few defenses against predators like these, and their numbers dropped dramatically.

This giant wētā is being handled at a nature reserve in New Zealand, where there are no mammal predators and the bugs are protected by law.

Giant wētās have bulky, armored bodies to protect them, and long antennae to sense their surroundings.

QUEEN ALEXANDRA'S BIRDWING

Butterflies are delicate creatures, and many species are fairly small. However, the Queen Alexandra's birdwing is anything but! This is the world's largest species of butterfly by wingspan, and it lives in the rainforests of Papua New Guinea. Its impressive size, and the beautiful colors of the male, once made it popular with collectors. But this butterfly is now protected by law, and it is illegal to buy or sell them.

FACT FILE

- **Scientific name:** *Ornithoptera alexandrae*
- **Class:** insect
- **Length:** females' wingspan up to 11 in (28 cm); males are smaller
- **Home:** tropical rainforests
- **Diet:** larvae eat leaves; adults feed on nectar

SIZE AND COLOR

The Queen Alexandra's birdwing is beautiful as well as big, though males and females look very different. Males have a yellow abdomen and iridescent greenish-blue wings with black veins. They are also smaller, with a wingspan that only reaches about 7.8 inches (20 cm). The females are bigger, with a wingspan that sometimes reaches up to 11 inches (28 cm)! However, their colors are dull compared to those of the flashy males.

A female Queen Alexandra's birdwing has brown wings with pale cream markings. Her larger body helps her to develop and carry her eggs.

STRIKING CATERPILLARS

Female birdwings lay large, yellow eggs on the leaves of the poisonous pipevine plant, which has large, thick leaves and starfish-shaped, purple flowers. When the caterpillars hatch out, they eat their eggshell and then start to feed on the plant's leaves, which makes their body toxic, too. They grow quickly, going through five different instars. They have fat bodies with red-tipped spikes and a distinctive white "saddle" marking about halfway along.

After their first molt, the caterpillar takes on the reddish-black color that it will keep until it pupates.

TIME TO CHANGE

By the time it is ready to pupate, a caterpillar can be up to 4.7 inches (12 cm) long. It travels until it finds a safe place, where it attaches itself with a belt of silk and sheds its skin, creating a casing called a chrysalis. Over the next six weeks or so it will change into an adult inside the chrysalis. The adult butterflies come out at dawn to feed on nectar from flowers, and to look for a mate. They can live as butterflies for three months or more.

Queen Alexandra's birdwing caterpillars usually pupate in a safe, sheltered spot, attached to a leaf or branch, high off the ground.

BIRDWINGS IN DANGER

These large butterflies have few natural predators, though they sometimes get caught in the webs of large spiders. However, the Queen Alexandra's birdwing is endangered. It lives only in a small region of rainforest in Papua New Guinea, and this habitat is shrinking as people clear the land to plant crops. The butterfly is also often illegally trapped by people who want to sell it to collectors. Laws are now in place to help protect these beautiful butterflies.

Male birdwings have striking colors and these butterflies are also attracted to brightly colored flowers. When they were discovered in 1906, the butterfly was named after Queen Alexandra, the wife of Britain's king at the time, Edward VII.

BRONZE ORANGE BUG

Also known as citrus bugs and stink bugs, these small insects are members of the "true bug" order (see page 9). Their mouthparts are adapted for piercing plants and sucking out the juices. And they have a fitting nickname, as they really do stink! When threatened, they can spray a smelly liquid at targets over 20 inches (50 cm) away. This protects the bug against other arthropods or birds who might want to eat it.

FACT FILE

- **Scientific name:** *Musgraveia sulciventris*
- **Class:** insect
- **Length:** up to 1 in (2.5 cm)
- **Home:** forests and orchards in eastern Australia
- **Diet:** plant juices

This female bronze orange bug has laid her eggs on a leaf. The eggs and the young nymphs that will hatch out are well camouflaged in green.

MANY COLORS

The bronze orange bug has two colors in its name, but during its life it goes through more than that! The eggs are pale green, and so are the nymphs that hatch out. As they grow and molt, the instars all have the same oval, flattened body shape, but they are different colors. First they turn bright orange, with a single black spot on the back. The next instar is a paler yellow, and the adult bug is dark bronze.

Starting life as a young green nymph (left), the orange instar (right) is now only a few molts from its adult form.

CITRUS PEST

For gardeners and citrus farmers in Australia, these bugs are real pests. They suck the juices from shoots and flowers, as well as from developing fruits, such as oranges, lemons, and limes. This damages the fruit, and a large infestation can destroy a whole crop. Some other insects, such as assassin bugs, will hunt them, but farmers often resort to pesticides to kill these insects.

The light patches on these citrus tree leaves show where this nymph and adult bug have been feeding on the plant's sap.

HUNTSMAN SPIDER

Huntsman spiders are found throughout Australia. These large, long-legged spiders often give people a fright when they scuttle out from behind a curtain. There are many different species of huntsman, but this is one of the most unusual, and is often known as the communal huntsman. These spiders are social animals, and can be found living together in large colonies.

FACT FILE

- **Scientific name:** *Delena cancerides*
- **Class:** arachnid
- **Length:** body up to 1.3 in (3.2 cm); leg span up to 6 in (15 cm)
- **Home:** wooded areas throughout Australia
- **Diet:** insects and other invertebrates

The legs of a huntsman spider spread out to the sides, giving them a crablike appearance. The flattened body shape is perfect for hiding beneath tree bark.

LIVING TOGETHER

A colony of communal huntsman spiders is ruled over by a female, and most of the rest of the colony are her offspring and descendants. The spiders live together, and they also share food with each other. In other spider species, the larger spiderlings often eat the smaller ones. But with communal huntsman, the older offspring help to feed the younger ones instead.

This artwork shows the scene you may encounter if you lift a layer of tree bark—a large colony of huntsman spiders, possibly up to 300!

COLONY POLITICS

Spiderlings in a communal huntsman colony have a better chance of reaching adulthood than many other spider species. However, once they reach the subadult phase of their life cycle, they must move out. The colony "queen" doesn't want adult females there who will compete with her, and she also doesn't want her own sons trying to mate with her. These spiders move out to either live on their own, or to start new colonies.

Female huntsman spiders look after their spiderlings for several weeks until they are ready to fend for themselves.

GUM-LEAF SKELETONIZER

Often, unremarkable-looking caterpillars turn into butterflies with striking looks. And sometimes it's the other way around! The gum-leaf skeletonizer lives in Australia and New Zealand. The moths of this species are small, dull, and browny-grey. With their long, venomous bristles and unusual headgear, it's the caterpillars that really stand out.

FACT FILE

- **Scientific name:** *Uraba lugens*
- **Class:** insect
- **Length:** caterpillars up to 0.8 in (2 cm); moths' wingspan up to 1.2 in (3 cm)
- **Home:** among eucalyptus trees in Australia and New Zealand
- **Diet:** larvae eat leaves; adults do not feed

WHAT'S WITH THE HAT?

The oddly-named gum-leaf skeletonizer has an even odder nickname: the Mad Hatterpillar! This is because each time the caterpillar molts, it doesn't shed its entire skin. The head casing of the old skin remains, and it sits on top of the caterpillar's head. Each time the caterpillar molts, the stack of "hats" gets bigger. Scientists think that this odd headgear might help to protect the caterpillar from predators, because it looks bigger and offers a false target.

A caterpillar might end up with a tall stack of "hats" on its head, each one bigger than the one above.

LEAF DESTROYER

The adult moths only live for about a week and do not feed. They lay their eggs on the underside of the leaves of eucalyptus trees and the caterpillars that hatch, eat the leaves in an unusual way. Instead of starting at the edge and chomping through the whole leaf, they only eat the top and bottom surfaces, leaving a network of veins behind, which look like the leaf's skeleton. Eucalyptus trees are also known as gum trees in Australia, so that's why these hungry caterpillars are called gum-leaf skeletonizers!

This adult moth (left) is well camouflaged against tree bark. Its offspring will feed hungrily on eucalyptus tree leaves (right).

The gum-leaf skeletonizer caterpillar has a unique look! Here you can see that, with each molt, the caterpillar's head has gotten bigger as it grows.

PEACOCK SPIDER

In the bird world, peacocks are known for their brilliantly colored tail fans, which they display to attract a mate. Peacock spiders get their name because they also use colors to impress the opposite sex. These spiders are tiny but beautiful, and there are many different species living in Australia, with a few in New Zealand and China as well.

FACT FILE

- **Scientific name:** genus *Maratus* (many species)
- **Class:** arachnid
- **Length:** body up to 0.2 in (5 mm), depending on species
- **Home:** many different environments, mainly in Australia
- **Diet:** insects and other spiders

MATING RITUAL

When a male peacock spider wants to attract the attention of a female, he finds a visible perch. He waves his third pair of legs, which are longer than the others, to gain her attention. Then he raises his abdomen which releases colorful flaps, and he wiggles to wave the whole thing back and forth. This dance shows off his colors to the best effect and can last for over an hour. Different species within the *Maratus* genus have different patterns of colorful markings.

In contrast to the male, the female is a dull brown color to stay camouflaged from predators.

COLORFUL JUMPERS

Peacock spiders belong to a larger group known as jumping spiders. These spiders are named for their jumping ability, but they also have amazing eyesight. Most spiders have eight eyes, but vision isn't their main way of finding prey—instead, they often use scent and vibrations. But jumping spiders have sharp eyes with good depth perception, which helps them accurately jump onto their prey.

All jumping spiders have four pairs of eyes, with two in the middle that are larger than the others.

Male peacock spiders use their bright colors for an elaborate courtship display to impress a female.

EUCALYPTUS LONGHORN BORER

Longhorn beetles are famous for their impressive antennae, which can be longer than the length of their body! There are about 35,000 species in this family, living all over the world. One of them, the eucalyptus longhorn borer, lives mainly in Australia, though it has been introduced to other areas, such as California, New Zealand, and southern Europe. It can live anywhere with a hot, dry climate—and plenty of eucalyptus trees!

FACT FILE

- **Scientific name:** *Phoracantha semipunctata*
- **Class:** insect
- **Length:** up to 1.2 in (3 cm)
- **Home:** hot, arid forest areas
- **Diet:** larvae eat wood; adults feed on pollen and nectar from trees

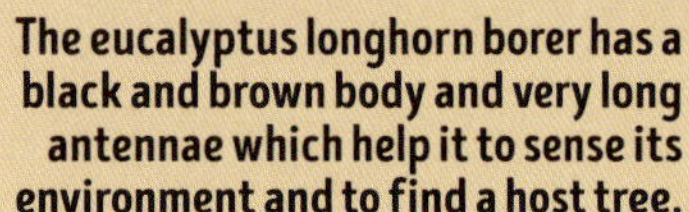

The eucalyptus longhorn borer has a black and brown body and very long antennae which help it to sense its environment and to find a host tree.

PROTECTIVE MEASURES

Damage caused by an infestation of eucalyptus longhorn borers is easy to see on the trunk of a tree. They tend to prefer drier trees as hosts, so keeping the trees watered is one way to keep the beetles at bay. Some people keep the beetle population under control by introducing a tiny black wasp that inserts its eggs inside the beetle's eggs. When the wasp larvae hatch, they eat up the beetle's eggs.

The beetle larvae can damage trees as they eat, leaving these lasting scars, and are usually seen as a pest.

LIFE IN A TREE

Eucalyptus longhorn borers lay their eggs beneath the bark of a tree. They choose trees that are dead or dying, often because of drought or natural disasters. When the eggs hatch, the larvae start to eat the underside of the tree's bark. As they grow bigger, they begin to eat the wood of the tree itself. Once they pupate, the adult beetles climb out of the tree. They now feed on pollen and sap as they look for a mate.

Eucalyptus trees are a favorite host plant of the longhorn borer, where the larvae feast on the bark.

RUFOUS NET-CASTING SPIDER

Spiders build many different kinds of webs. Some spin spiral orbs with thin, sticky strands for catching prey. Others build silken tunnels or trapdoors. Net-casting spiders do something different—they spin a small, netlike web, then hold it with their legs and use it to snare prey. There are species in many parts of the world, but the rufous net-casting spider lives in Australia.

FACT FILE

- **Scientific name:** *Asianopis subrufa*
- **Class:** arachnid
- **Length:** males' body up to 0.6 in (1.5 cm); females up to 1 in (2.5 cm)
- **Home:** open woodland
- **Diet:** insects and other arthropods

OGRE FACE?

The rufous net-casting spider belongs to a group often known as "ogre-faced spiders," because of their scary-looking faces. "Rufous" means reddish and refers to the color of the females. Both males and females have long, thin bodies, but females are larger. Males are darker in color, with light and dark gray stripes, and often have thinner legs. Their body shape allows them to hide in foliage, where they could be mistaken for a stick if they stand still.

Net-casting spiders have eight eyes, but two are much larger than the rest, helping them to see in low light.

HUNTING WITH NETS

At night, a rufous net-casting spider spins a rectangular web about the size of a postage stamp. Then it gets into position, dangling from a thread of silk over a place where prey animals are likely to walk past. When it spots prey, it stretches the web open and lunges. It quickly wraps the prey in its sticky net and bites it. The spider has excellent eyesight, even at night, and can catch prey on the ground or in the air.

This female has used her net to capture a jumping spider, which is now fully entangled in a mesh of silk.

This rufous net-casting spider is waiting for unsuspecting prey to pass by, so it can pounce on it with its net.

SYDNEY FUNNEL-WEB SPIDER

Australia is famous for being home to many dangerous animals, such as the saltwater crocodile, the great white shark, and venomous snakes like the inland taipan. However, one of the continent's deadliest animals is much smaller—it's the Sydney funnel-web spider! This spider is found in forests and urban areas in the southeastern coastal regions, near the city of Sydney.

FACT FILE

- **Scientific name:** *Atrax robustus*
- **Class:** arachnid
- **Length:** males' body up to 1 in (2.5 cm); females up to 1.4 in (3.5 cm)
- **Home:** forests and urban areas in southeast Australia
- **Diet:** insects and other small invertebrates

SPECIAL WEBS

A Sydney funnel-web spider has two fingerlike spinnerets at the end of its abdomen, which produce silk for its web. The tube-shaped web lies inside a burrow dug into the ground. It is wider at the entrance and then gradually narrows, like a funnel. The web can be anywhere from 8–24 inches (20-60 cm) long. Sydney funnel-web spiders usually choose moist soil for their burrows, such as beneath rocks and fallen trees. They also build them beneath houses or in compost heaps.

This is the entrance to a funnel-web spider's burrow—the only part that is visible from aboveground.

TIME TO EAT

The funnel-shaped webs often have trip-lines spreading out over the ground. When prey walks across the trip lines, the spider rushes out of its burrow and attacks with its fangs. Sydney funnel-web spiders eat insects, such as beetles or cockroaches, as well as snails and millipedes. They can also attack larger prey, including frogs and lizards. Once it's bitten its prey, the spider drags it back into the burrow to eat it.

This Sydney funnel-web spider is emerging from its burrow because its web has been disturbed, perhaps by prey that would make a tasty meal.

AGGRESSIVE BITE

Sydney funnel-web spiders have large fangs and powerful venom, and they often bite repeatedly, or hang on until removed. They are aggressive and will lash out when they feel threatened. What's worse, they often end up in homes or gardens where they are likely to come into contact with humans. A bite from a funnel-web spider must be treated immediately in a hospital.

In Australia, people are advised to shake out their clothing and shoes before putting them on, especially if they've been left outside.

When threatened, a Sydney funnel-web spider will rear up onto its hind legs and display its fangs.

SAVING LIVES

Because the bite of a Sydney funnel-web spider can be fatal to humans, scientists have worked hard to develop an antivenom. To do this, they need venom from the spiders themselves. The Australian Reptile Park in Sydney has set up a collection program. People bring them spiders or egg sacs that they find. Then they raise the spiders and "milk" them for their venom.

The venom collected from the spider's fangs is used to make a lifesaving treatment for funnel-web bites.

HIBISCUS HARLEQUIN BUG

Also known as the cotton harlequin bug, this small, brightly colored bug is found in cities, farms, and coastal areas of eastern and northern Australia. It is part of the jewel bug family and has the same metallic sheen as many of its relatives. The bugs feed on plants, such as cotton and hibiscus, using their mouthparts to pierce the shoots and then suck out the sap.

FACT FILE

- **Scientific name:** *Tectocoris diophthalmus*
- **Class:** insect
- **Length:** up to 0.8 in (2 cm)
- **Home:** wooded areas in Australia
- **Diet:** plant sap

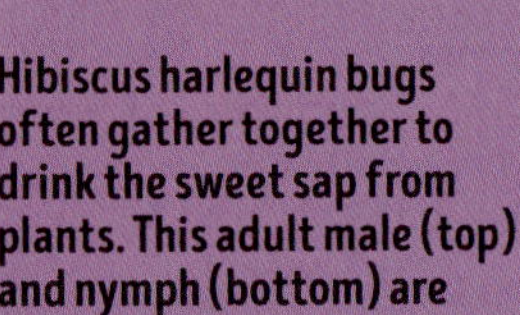

Hibiscus harlequin bugs often gather together to drink the sweet sap from plants. This adult male (top) and nymph (bottom) are feeding on Jatropha fruit.

DIFFERENT COLORS

These bugs come in several colors, depending on their sex and stage in the life cycle. In fact, scientists once thought the color variations were several different species! Females are mostly orange, often with blue spots, while males are mainly blue. The immature nymphs can also be different colors, changing with each molt. Scientists think that this variation might help to protect them from birds that try to eat them.

These photos show some of the varying colors, from the bright orange female and blue male to young nymphs that are green and orange.

STANDING GUARD

Many insect species lay their eggs and then leave forever. However, the hibiscus harlequin bug does things differently! The female lays a clutch of eggs in a cylindrical shape, surrounding a small branch or stem of the host plant. Then she stays with the eggs, guarding them until they hatch. Predators are less likely to eat eggs that are guarded. In a study, for example, scientists found that four times as many eggs hatched safely when they were guarded than those left on their own.

This female is carefully guarding her eggs. Once they hatch, she will stay with the nymphs for a few days.

CATHEDRAL TERMITE

Many bugs build homes for themselves. These can be simple underground burrows, wispy spiderwebs, or intricate nests filled with hexagonal cells for raising young. But perhaps no insect home is more impressive than the mounds built by the cathedral termite. These immense structures dot the landscape in northern Australia, and they can reach heights of over 26 ft (8 m)!

FACT FILE

- **Scientific name:** *Nasutitermes triodiae*
- **Class:** insect
- **Length:** soldiers up to 0.2 in (4.5 mm)
- **Home:** dry areas of northern Australia
- **Diet:** grass

MOUND BUILDERS

Cathedral termite mounds are marvels of engineering. The termites use a mixture of mud, plant matter, saliva, and feces to build them up to imposing heights. Within the mounds are a number of hollow, vertical tubes connected by branching tunnels. To keep the termites at a comfortable temperature, the mound's shape and orientation means that one side is always shaded as the Sun rises and falls, and when the Sun is directly overhead, only the pointed top receives direct sunlight.

This photo and artwork show the outside and inside of a cathedral termite mound, with its various tunnels and air vents.

KEEPING COMFORTABLE

Inside the termite mound, the hollow tubes act like an air-conditioning system, allowing cooler air from the base of the mound to circulate to the top, where it is warmer. The termites use some of their chambers to store grass. Unlike many other termite species, which eat wood, cathedral termites eat grasses, which they bring back to the mound as a food supply. While workers build and maintain the mound, specialized soldier termites protect the colony, and the queen in particular, who lays all the eggs. Soldiers can shoot a special liquid out of their snout to repel invaders, such as ants.

These soldier termites of a closely-related species have rushed to their queen's defense as a form of protection, because their nest has been cut open.

These cathedral termites are emerging from a huge mound—the cathedral-like tower that gives the species its common name.

GIANT PILL MILLIPEDE

You'd be forgiven for thinking that this creature is just a supersized woodlouse. The giant pill millipede has a similar body shape, but it's in a completely different group! Woodlice are crustaceans, like crabs and lobsters, but pill millipedes are more closely related to centipedes. There are many species living across the southern hemisphere, but the genus *Procyliosoma* is native to New Zealand and Australia.

FACT FILE

- **Scientific name:** genus *Procyliosoma* (several species)
- **Class:** myriapod
- **Length:** up to 2 in (5 cm)
- **Home:** moist habitats in New Zealand and Australia
- **Diet:** dead plant and animal matter

CURLING UP

Pill millipedes get their name because of their habit of curling up into a tight ball when threatened. The armored plates on their back fit perfectly into each other, creating a ball shape so tightly sealed that predators can't uncurl it. When rolled up, giant pill millipedes are the size of a large cherry. Once they uncurl, they move about the forest floor, looking for decaying plant and animal matter to eat.

This giant pill millipede has curled up to sleep during the day, and will wake up at night to feed.

LITTLE AND LARGE

Giant pill millipedes have fewer body segments than other millipedes. They have up to 13 body segments and 23 pairs of legs, depending on the sex and species. However, scientists have recently found a different Australian millipede that sets a record for the most segments! *Eumillipes persephone* was discovered in 2021 deep underground, in drill holes created by mining companies. The largest specimen was a female with 330 body segments and 1,306 legs!

***Eumillipes persephone* is the first known millipede to have over 1,000 legs, although its length is just 3.7 inches (9.5 cm).**

Giant pill millipedes feed on moss and other organic matter found in leaf litter.

WEAVER ANT

Have you ever built a paper model, using glue to hold the pieces together? Weaver ants make their nests in a similar way, but they use leaves instead of paper, and produce the glue themselves! These aggressive ants live in large colonies of up to 500,000 individuals and are found in the tropical forests of Australia and Southeast Asia. They live and build their nests in trees.

FACT FILE

- **Scientific name:** *Oecophylla smaragdina*
- **Class:** insect
- **Length:** workers up to 0.4 in (10 mm); queens up to 1 in (2.5 cm)
- **Home:** tropical forests of northern Australia and Southeast Asia
- **Diet:** insects and other invertebrates as well as honeydew

BUILDING A NEST

Weaver ants have an unusual method of building a nest. First, a group of workers finds a likely location in a tree. Then, they line up along the edge of a leaf and work together to pull it toward another leaf. Then other worker ants step in, carrying larvae in their mouths. Each larva produces fine, sticky silk from its mouth. They use these larvae like tubes of glue, letting their silk fasten the two leaves together.

These weaver ants are working together to build a nest (left). The ants use the sticky silk from larvae as a type of glue (right).

ANT IMITATORS

One species of jumping spider has evolved a body shape that mimics that of the weaver ant. Its body segments are thin in places, giving it the appearance of having a separate head, thorax, and abdomen. Two black patches on the head look like an ant's large eyes. These spiders live among the same plants as the weaver ants. Potential predators know that weaver ants are aggressive and taste bad, so by resembling them the jumping spiders stay safe.

Count the legs! This eight-legged creature is a spider, not an ant.

Weaver ants capture prey they find near their nest. Because they work together, they can capture prey that is bigger than themselves, like this fly.

ANTARCTICA

At the southernmost part of our planet, there is a land of ice and snow. Antarctica is a huge continent, but its freezing temperatures mean that very little life can survive here. Animals thrive in the cold, nutrient-rich oceans that surround Antarctica, but hardly any plants grow in the interior of the continent. This lack of food makes it difficult for any animals to survive, but a few do.

Grasses and mosses grow along the coast where it's warmer, attracting flies, midges, and springtails.

The nutrient-rich ocean sustains seals and seabirds, and the bugs they feed on, such as krill and sea spiders.

The Geographic South Pole is a freezing, snowy, barren place, where it also stays dark for half the year.

There is one reliable source of heat in Antarctica—Mount Erebus has been erupting for more than 50 years!

The McMurdo Dry Valleys are one of the driest places on Earth, but springtails and mites survive here.

Lake Vostok is hidden beneath thick ice, and scientists have discovered single-celled organisms in its waters.

MAP KEY

Polar Ice

Ice Shelf

ANTARCTIC MIDGE

The Antarctic midge is tiny, but it is still the largest animal native to Antarctica that lives completely on land. Although midges are a type of fly, this species has no wings so cannot take to the air. It can survive in freezing temperatures by burrowing into soil. In fact, it needs to stay cold and cannot survive in temperatures above 50 °F (10 °C)! These midges spend most of their two-year life cycle as larvae, where they feed on decaying organic matter. Adults emerge in spring and summer and only live for a week or two.

This Antarctic midge is sheltering in moss, away from the wind.

FACT FILE

- **Scientific name:** *Belgica antarctica*
- **Class:** insect
- **Length:** up to 0.2 in (6 mm)
- **Home:** Antarctic tundra, burrows in moist soil
- **Diet:** larvae eat algae and fungi; adults do not eat

SPRINGTAIL

Springtails are arthropods with six legs, but they are not considered to be insects. Unlike insects, springtails have their mouthparts tucked inside their head. They also have a special tail-like structure called a furcula that helps them jump up to 6.3 inches (16 cm) in the air. They live in huge numbers in soil all over the world, and a handful of species live in Antarctica. This particular springtail has special proteins that keep it from freezing in extreme temperatures.

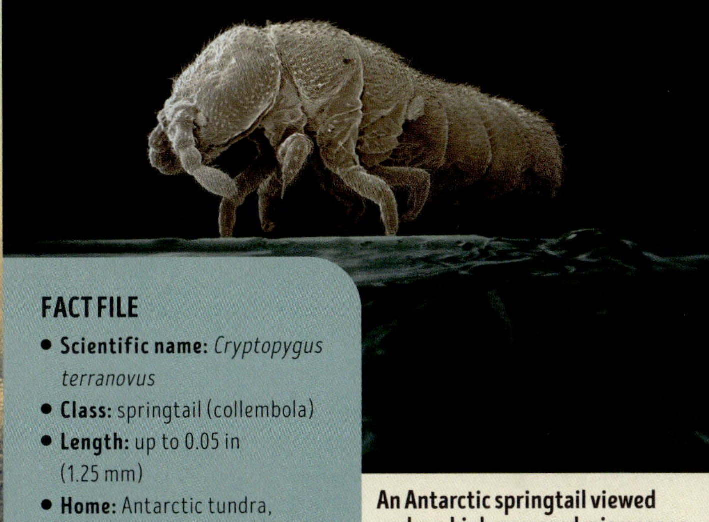

An Antarctic springtail viewed under a high-powered microscope.

FACT FILE

- **Scientific name:** *Cryptopygus terranovus*
- **Class:** springtail (collembola)
- **Length:** up to 0.05 in (1.25 mm)
- **Home:** Antarctic tundra, often under stones
- **Diet:** decaying organic matter

DUNG FLY

The Antarctic coast and surrounding islands are home to several species of small fly. This particular species is a member of a family called the lesser dung flies. They are tiny and dull colored, with short antennae and no wings. The larvae graze on microbes, while the adults feed on the dung of mammals, such as seals, that live in the area.

This dung fly has been magnified many times by a high-powered microscope.

FACT FILE

- **Scientific name:** *Anatalanta aptera*
- **Class:** insect
- **Length:** unknown
- **Home:** Antarctic tundra
- **Diet:** dung

SEA SPIDER

Sea spiders aren't actually spiders—or even arachnids! These arthropods live in oceans all over the world. Most are small, but this Antarctic species is bigger, and while most species have four pairs of legs, this one has five. Sea spiders use their legs for paddling as well as walking, and pierce their prey with their tubular proboscis to suck out the insides.

Sea spiders walk in search of prey, such as worms and anemones.

FACT FILE

- **Scientific name:** *Decolopoda australis*
- **Class:** pycnogonida
- **Length:** leg span over 8 in (20 cm)
- **Home:** Antarctic waters
- **Diet:** soft-bodied sea creatures

GLOSSARY

ABDOMEN A body part found in some arthropods. An insect's body is divided into three segments—head, thorax, abdomen—with the abdomen being the rearmost, while an arachnid's body is divided into an abdomen and a cephalothorax.

ANTENNAE A pair of slender, segmented sensory organs found on the heads of insects, myriapods, and crustaceans, which help them to sense the world around them. Arachnids do not have antennae.

ANTIVENOM An antidote to the venom produced by an insect, arachnid, or other animal. Sometimes called antivenin.

APPENDAGE A part of an animal's body that sticks out from the main part of the body, such as a limb.

ARTHROPODS A large group within the animal kingdom that includes insects, arachnids, myriapods, and other animals with jointed legs and a tough exoskeleton.

CAMOUFLAGE The use of shape or coloration to allow a living thing to conceal itself from other animals. This can involve blending into the background, mimicking the appearance of an object, such as a twig, or looking like a different and more dangerous animal.

CEPHALOTHORAX The fused head and thorax body segment found in arachnids and crustaceans.

CHRYSALIS The hardened outer layer of a butterfly during its pupa stage. The chrysalis protects the insect inside as it completes its metamorphosis into an adult butterfly.

CLIMATE CHANGE The significant and long-lasting change in Earth's climate and weather patterns. Modern climate change is due to human activity, such as burning fossil fuels. Climate change often makes it harder for plants and animals to survive in their environment.

COCOON A protective covering made of silk and sometimes other materials, in which moths and some other types of insects complete their metamorphosis.

COLONY A group of animals of the same species that live in the same place and work together to help the group survive, such as by building a home, finding food, or defending the nest.

CRUSTACEAN A member of the large group of arthropods that includes crabs, lobsters, and woodlice.

DECOMPOSITION The breaking down of living material once it has died, so that the nutrients it contains can be recycled.

ELYTRA The hardened forewings of beetles and some other types of insects, which protect the more delicate flying wings beneath.

ENTOMOLOGIST A scientist who studies insects.

ENZYME A natural chemical produced in the cells of living things that helps the body by speeding up chemical reactions.

EVOLVE To undergo physical changes, so that later generations are different from their ancestors in ways that make them better suited to survive in their environment.

EXCRETED Expelled from the body, such as in the form of urine or solid waste.

EXOSKELETON The hard outer covering of an arthropod, which protects the soft body parts inside. Arthropods shed their exoskeleton when it becomes too small, and the new, larger exoskeleton beneath then hardens to take its place.

FERTILIZE To fuse the reproductive cells of a female (egg) and a male (sperm) to produce a new offspring that will have characteristics of both parents.

FORAGE To move around in search of food to eat, usually plants.

GENES The basic building blocks by which traits are passed down from parents to their offspring. Genes contain instructions that tell the body how to grow and develop.

GENUS A rank in taxonomy that sits below family but above species. Animals (or plants) of the same genus share many similarities, but they cannot usually reproduce successfully together unless they are also of the same species.

HOST PLANT The plant on which an animal lives and feeds.

INFESTATION The state of being overrun by pests or parasites, which can cause damage. Plants are often infested by insects.

INSECTICIDE A chemical used to kill insects. Most insecticides are made in factories, but some natural materials are also used.

INSTAR The stage between each molt in an arthropod's life.

IRIDESCENCE A shimmering, rainbowlike visual effect caused when light refracts from a material in a particular way. Iridescence makes an object appear to change color when viewed from different angles.

LARVA The young form of some types of insects and other arthropods, which looks different from the adult and will undergo metamorphosis before taking its adult form.

MANDIBLES A pair of mouthparts found in arthropods, used for biting, cutting, or holding food. Sometimes described as jaws.

MATE A partner of the opposite sex that an animal can pair with to produce offspring. When they do this, it is called mating.

METAMORPHOSIS The process by which an animal changes its body shape in stages as it grows. Many arthropods undergo metamorphosis, which can be either complete or incomplete.

MIGRATE To move from one location to another, often on a seasonal basis to find food.

MILKY WAY The galaxy that is home to our Sun and Solar System as well as billions of other stars. On dark nights it can be seen as a ribbon of light in the sky, which some animals use to navigate.

MUTATION A random change in a gene that produces a new and different trait. Some mutations can be passed on to a living thing's offspring.

NATIVE Naturally occurring in a particular place or environment.

NOCTURNAL Mainly active at night.

NYMPH The juvenile form of some insects, which will undergo incomplete metamorphosis before becoming an adult. Nymphs usually look similar to the adult form, though they may lack wings and be unable to mate.

PARASITE A living thing that survives by living on or inside a host organism, which usually causes harm to the host organism.

PEDIPALPS A pair of appendages found at the front of spiders, scorpions, and some other arthropods, on their cephalothorax. Pedipalps are used for many things, including sensing, digging, holding prey, and attracting a mate.

POLLINATE To transfer pollen from the male part of a flower to the female part, either of the same flower or of a different one. Pollination is necessary for the formation of seeds and is often carried out by insects, such as bees, as they feed.

PREDATOR An animal that hunts and eats other animals for food.

PROBOSCIS The tubular arrangement of mouthparts in some insects, such as butterflies and bees, which allows them to suck up liquid food.

PUPA The stage of the life cycle of some insects during which the body shape changes to that of an adult. During this stage, the insect does not move around much and usually stays safe inside a hardened outer case.

PUPATE To enter the pupa stage of the life cycle.

QUARANTINING Placing a living thing, such as a plant or animal, in isolation to prevent the spread of a disease or pest.

REGURGITATE To bring up undigested or partly digested food from inside the body, usually in order for adults to feed it to their young.

ROOST To gather together with other members of the species to rest, often perched on a tree.

SPECIES A rank in taxonomy that sits below genus. Animals of the same species are very similar to each other and can breed and produce young.

SPINNERET An organ found in some insect larvae and many spiders, which is used to produce silk for making webs or cocoons.

STEPPE A large area of flat, unforested grassland in southeastern Europe and parts of Asia.

SUBSPECIES A smaller group within a species.

SURFACE TENSION A phenomenon caused by the attraction of water molecules that results in the formation of a "skin" at the water's surface, allowing small objects, such as insects, to rest on water without sinking.

TAXONOMY A system for naming and organizing plants and animals into groups that share similar qualities.

THORAX One of the three body segments of an insect. The thorax lies between the head and the abdomen.

TOXIC Poisonous and capable of causing harm if eaten or ingested.

TOXINS Toxic chemicals produced inside the body of a living organism.

TRANSLUCENT Partly see-through.

TUNDRA A vast, flat, treeless region in which the subsoil is permanently frozen.

VENOMOUS Producing a toxin within the body that can be delivered by means of a bite or sting.

INDEX

PICTURE CREDITS

PHOTOGRAPHY CREDITS

Key l=left, r=right, t=top, b=bottom, c=center, bg=background.

Cover: Shutterstock/Creative Commons.
Shutterstock: p1 Photografiero, p2-3 Oasishifi, p4-5 Romolo Tavani, p6 (b) Nikolas Gregor, p7 (t) Melnikov Dmitriy, p7 (b) NeagoneFo, p8-9 (bg), p11 (ml), p75 (bl) and p106 (bg) Ernie Cooper, p8 (ml) and p153 (bg) frank60, p8 (bl) Christoph Scholz, p9 (tr) Plutonian_p, p9 (br) I Wayan Sumatika, p10-11 (bg) David Pineda Svenske, p10 (br) Daniel Prudek, p11 (br) symbiot, p12-13 (bg) Robert Sanjeev Ross, p12 (t) nujames10, p12 (b) and p41 (bg) Darkdiamond67, p12 (b) IrinaK, p13 (tr) and p127 (bl) Lauren Suryanata, p14 (t), p38 (t), p60 (t), p86 (t), p112 (t), p136 (t) and p154 (t) Peter Hermes Furian, p14 (tr) Troutnut, p14 (tl) Matthew James Ferguson, p14 (mr) Scenic Corner, p14 (ml) 86Eric_Anthony_Mischke 86, p14 (br) and p112 (br) Teo Tarras, p14 (bl) Traveller70, p15 (bg) Share, p16 (bg) Jamie Spensley, p16 (l) Randall Saltys, p16 (b) Physics_joe, p17 (bg), p17 (ml), p19 (bg), p24 (bg) and p30 (br) Jay Ondreicka, p18 (bg) G Talley, p18 (mr) Matt Jeppson, p18 (br) BonnieMarquette, p19 (ml) KPixMining, p19 (bl), p69 (ml) and p84 (b) Tomasz Klejdysz, p19 (br) Sarah2, p20 (ml) Mathias Dezetter, p20 (bl) Yusak priyanto, p21 (bg) Lutsenko Oleksandr, p22-23 (bg) Pedro Luna, p24 (m) and p26-27 (bg) Mark Kostich, p25 (m) Rostislav Stefanek, p25 (b) Mladen Mitrinovic, p27 (br) Nikolay Kurzenko, p28 (bg) Therese15, p28 (ml) K Quinn Ferris, p28 (b) Malachi Jacobs, p29 (ml) Dennis MacDonald, p30 (bg) j_fredz, p31 (br) JossK, p32-33 (bg) Neil Aronson, p32 (bl) Piper333, p32 (tr) and p35 (bl) Sari Oneal, p33 (ml) Manuel Balesteri, p33 (br) and p156-157 JHVEPhoto, p34 (bg) Kevin Collison, p34 (bl) and p34 (br) Cathy Keifer, p35 (bg) samray, p35 (br) Gerry Bishop, p36 (bg) Anest, p36 (mr) Rasmuscool99, p37 (mr) Niney Azman, p38 (tr) ecuadorplanet, p38 (tl) Mathew Risley, p38 (mr) Kelly Richter, p38 (br) Roberto Tetsuo Okamura, p38 (bl) PositiveTravelArt, p38 (b) Jennifer Stone, p39 (bg) and p89 (bg) Petr Muckstein, p40 (bg) Salparadis, p40 (m) SoFlo Shots, p40 (btl) SIMON SHIM, p40 (btr) and p80 (bg) fendercapture, p40 (bbl) and p140-141 (bg) Russell Marshall, p40 (bbr) Eddy Surahyo, p44 (bg) wesleylilin, p45 (ml) Sunux, p47 (bg) RudiErnst, p48-49 (bg) feathercollector, p48 (b) and p49 (mr) fukushima insectarium, p50 (bm) INTREEGUE Photography, p50 (br) SL-Photographer, p51 (bl) Sinhyu Photographer, p52 (bg) William2023, p52 (mr) Allen Lara Gonzalez, p54-55 (bg), p54 (br) and p106 (bl) Milan Zygmunt, p55 (tr) and p120 (bg) Wirestock Creators, p55 (mr) asawinimages, p56 (bg) hagit berkovich, p56 (tr) and p56 (bl) Dr Morley Read, p57 (mr) amskad, p58 (bl) guentermanaus, p59 (bg) Jody., p59 (br) Keith Hider, p60 (mlt) Aleksander Bolbot, p60 (mlb) Helen Hotson, p60 (mr) Sergey Demo SVDPhoto, p60 (bl) elis.dreamer, p60 (bm) Max Topchii, p60 (br) Khorzhevska, p61 (bg) and p80 (ml) HWall, p62 (bg) WildMedia, p62 (mr) Carl Mckie, p62 (br) Kriachko Oleksii, p63 (mr) Igor Nikushin, p63 (br) Alen thien, p64-65 (bg) tividan, p64 (bl) sophiecat, p65 (tl) and p65 (mr) and p76 (b) Henrik Larsson, p65 (br) InsectWorld, p66 (ml) Dan Gabriel Atanasie, p67 (bg) Lubomir Dajc, p68 (bg) and p160 Piotr Guttmeyer, p68 (bl) Dadang Eka Pradana, p69 (bg) and p132-133 (bg) David Havel, p70-71 (bg) Robert Schneider, p71 (tr) Mirko Graul, p71 (ml) Hakim Graphy, p71 (br) Dirk Daniel Mann, p72 (bg) Dirk Ercken, p72 (ml) slowmotiongli, p72 (mr) Martin Pelanek, p73 (bg), p124 (ml), p146 (bm) and p146 (br) Protasov AN, p73 (bl) Petrovicheva Mariia, p73 (br) khunkornStudio, p74 (bg) Bildagentur Zoonar GmbH, p74 (ml) and p113 (bg) R. Maximiliane, p74 (mr) Meik, p75 (bg) Maleo, p75 (br) Muddy knees, p77 (t) and p82 (b) IanRedding, p78 (bl) Somyot Mali-ngam, p78 (br) Dmitry Fch, p79 (bg) Ondrej Michalek, p79 (ml) Christos Sallas, p79 (mr) Macronatura.es, p80 (mr) My Angel L.A. Images, p81 (bg) Lukas Jonaitis, p81 (ml) Pete Mella, p82 (ml) Subas Chandra Mahato, p83 (tr) Ihor Hvozdetskyi, p83 (br) dimid_86, p84 (bg) Przemyslaw Muszynski, p85 (bg) Pavel Krasensky, p85 (br) and p103 (tl) Holger Kirk, p86 (tl) Atosan, p86 (tr) Framalicious, p86 (ml) Cocos. Bounty, p86 (mr) Simon Dannhauer, p86 (bl) EcoPrint, p86 (br) Sean Newbery, p87 (bg) Dennis van de Water, p87 (ml) Artush, p88 (bg) akids.photo.graphy, p88 (bl) De19, p88 (br) Merih Salmaz, p90-91 (bg), p90 (ml), p91 (br) and p124 (bg) Mark Brandon, p91 (tl) and p138 (b) Ireneusz Waledzik, p92 (bg) D. Kucharski K. Kucharska, p92 (bl) and p131 (bg) Marek R. Swadzba, p93 (bg) AlisLuch, p94 (bg) Vaclav Sebek, p94 (ml) TairA, p95 (bg) Dave Montreuil, p95 (ml) Fabio Sacchi, p97 (bg) Cornel Constantin, p97 (bl) olko1975, p98 (bg) A. Kehinde, p99 (br) Fabian Plock, p100 (bg) Mpho Seanego, p100 (bl) Ondrej Prosicky, p100 (br) Rainer Lesniewski, p101 (bg) Alex Stemmer, p101 (br) Eaknarong Nonthapha, p102-103 (bg) Boris Edelmann, p102 (ml) and p103 (tr) Mikhail Gnatkovskiy, p103 (mr) Olha Solodenko, p103 (br) Fabio Lamanna, p104 (bg) Milton Buzon, p104 (ml) Tacio Philip Sansonovski, p104 (mr) PongMoji, p105 (bg) BBA Photography, p105 (ml) Jana Nechvatal, p105 (mr) Destinys Agent, p106 (mr) McGraw, p108-109 (bg) Jane Rix, p108 (ml) Vladimir Wrangel, p109 (mr) Jen Watson, p110 (bg) torook, p110 (ml) and p111 (bl) Guillermo Guerao Serra, p111 (bg) morslasdert, p112 (tl) Emjay Smith, p112 (tm) Aureliy, p112 (tr) Andrei Stepanov, p112 (mr) Mr. Aleksandr Lenkov, p112 (bl) Prawat Thananithaporn, p113 (mr) TY Lim, p114 (bg) Kawin Jiaranaisakul, p114 (bl) Zuzha, p115 (bg) and p126 (br) Pong Wira, p115 (ml) zaidi razak, p116-117 (bg) Ava Peattie, p117 (mr) and p117 (br) Vijin Varghese, p118 (bg) BirdShutterB, p118 (ml) Catherine Eckert, p119 (ml) W. de Vries, p120 (br) Bdp Studio, p121 (bg) Lapis2380, p121 (bl) yosuyosun, p122-123 (bg) Ken Kojima, p122 (bl) Tatiana.Sidorova, p123 (tr) Hank Asia, p124 (mr) David Carillet, p125 (ml) tempisch, p125 (br) Linn Currie, p126-127 (bg) monster_code, p127 (tr) Sebastian Janicki, p127 (mr) Jamikorn Sooktaramorn, p129 (br) khlungcenter, p130 (bg) and p158-159 IRINA RAIDO, p131 (ml) nexusby, p131 (br) Sanit Fuangnakhon, p132 (br) MyImages – Micha, p133 (tr) Wiyada Jaroenkhan, p133 (mr) Marcel Derweduwen, p133 (bl) Upen supendi, p134 (bg) yod 67, p134 (mr) assoonas, p135 (bg) Marco Maggesi, p136 (ml) kwest, p136 (mrt) Ethan Daniels, p136 (mrb) Molly Brown NZ, p136 (bl) RugliG, p136 (bm) Michael Bluschke, p136 (br) synthetic, p138 (bg) Danita Delimont, p138 (ml) Aming Dolvin Jennefer, p139 (ml) Nima, p142 (bg) Cassandra Madsen, p142 (mr) Connie Pinson, p145 (mr) Kristian Bell, p148-149 (bg) and p149 (mr) Ken Griffiths, p150 (bg) Wong Gunkid, p150 (bl) Mikulas P, p150 (bml) Wiwik sisto, p150 (bmr) SIbangbrang Kasarung, p153 (mr) O partime photo, p153 (bl) NuayLub, p154 (bg) DidGason, p154 (ml) Uwe Bauer, p154 (mrt) NicoElNino, p154 (bl) ENVIROSENSE, p154 (bm) Dale Lorna Jacobsen, p155 (bg) Jeff Amantea.
Adobe Stock: p149 (tr) Sahara Frost.
Alamy: p6-7 (bg) Frank Bienewald, p15 (b) Mark Lehigh, p21 (bl) mauritius images GmbH, p22 (br) and p94 (mr) Ivan Kuzmin, p23 (tr) Minden Pictures, p24 (b) Jeff March, p25 (bg) and p31 (bl) Nature Picture Library, p29 (bg) and p30 (bl) piemags/nature, p29 (b) Jit Lim, p31 (bg) Clarence Holmes Wildlife, p39 (br) BIOSPHOTO, p41 (bl), p78 (bg) and p143 (bg) blickwinkel, p41 (br) Survivalphotos, p42-43 (bg) and p43 (tr) Michael Durham/Minden Pictures, p45 (bg), p45 (br) and p47 (ml) Piotr Naskrecki/Minden Pictures, p46 (mr) Mathias Putze, p46 (br) Wildlife World, p53 (bg) Redmond O. Durrell, p53 (br) Mark Moffett/Minden Pictures, p54 (ml) Daniel Heuclin Biosphoto, p57 (bg) Carver Mostardi, p58 (bg) and p77 (b) Les Gibbon, p61 (ml) Ã–ZGÃœR Kerem Bulur, p61 (mr) and p89 (br) Hakan Soderholm, p63 (bg) Michael Durham, p66 (bg) Dave Bevan, p66 (bl) Nigel Housden, p76-77 (bg) Bill Coster IN, p85 (bl) and p153 (mr) Emanuele Biggi, p87 (mr) Alexandra Laube, p93 (mr) Marcos Veiga, p95 (mr) William Attard McCarthy, p96 (bg) and p96 (mr) Solvin Zankl, p98 (br) Frank Deschandol & Philippe Sabine/Biosphoto, p99 (bl) Ray Wilson, p107 (bg) Dave Marsden, p111 (br) Media Drum World, p121 (br) Rudmer Zwerver, p122 (br) Sergio Yoneda, p137 (bg) Mitsuaki Iwago/Minden Pictures, p137 (br) Bill Bachman, p140 (mr) Michael Workman, p140 (br) and p141 (tl) Reinhard Dirscherl, p142 (ml) Andrew Trevor-Jones, p144 (ml) Denis Crawford, p146 (bg) Brian & Sophia Fuller, p147 (mr) cbstockfoto, p151 (bg) Juniors Bildarchiv GmbH, p152 (bg) fishHook Photography.
Creative Commons: p11 (tr) Meghan Cassidy, p13 (br), p15 (l) Andy, p17 (mr) Dehaan, p20 (bg) Ryan Hodnett, p21 (br), p23 (mr) Bruce Marlin, p23 (bl) Jacy Lucier, p36 (ml), p37 (bg) Judy Gallagher, p37 (ml) WanderingMogwai, p42 (mr) TheCoz, p43 (ml) Sandford Porter, p44 (br) Biologoandre, p46 (bg) Syrio, p47 (brt) and p47 (brb) Harald Süpfle, p48 (ml) Novita Estiti, p49 (tr) Hans Hillewaert, p52 (br) Bernard DUPONT, p55 (br) Snakecollector, p58 (ml) Anaxibia, p59 (ml) Pato Novoa, p67 (mr) Thue, p70 (bl) Jessica Lawrence, p76 (m) Noor MAF, Parnell RS, Grant BS, p81 (mr) gailhampshire, p82-83 (bg) Frank Vassen, p84 (ml) Janet Graham, p91 (mr) Dclees, p92 (br) Lepidopteron, p97 (br) Katya, p98 (bl) Alandmanson, p101 (mr) Hirvenkürpa, p107 (ml) Olga Ernst, p107 (mr) George Chernilevsky, p109 (tl) AtelierMonpli, p113 (br) Hectonichus, p114 (br) and p117 (tl) Drägüs, p115 (mr) Zarrizkem, p118 (br) Gilles San Martin, p118 (mr) Toby Young, p119 (bg) Zivya, p119 (mr) Fastily (talk), p123 (br) Takahashi, p125 (bg) Bay Lee's 8 Legged Art, p128 (bg) Rison Thumboor, p129 (bg) Rob Knell, p130 (bl) Pjt56, p135 (bl) Didier Descouens, p137 (bl) Greg Hume, p139 (bg) Dylan van Winkel, p139 (mr) jokertrekker, p142 (br) Jan Anderson, p143 (br) Don Horne, p144 (m) and p144 (mr) Donald Hobern, p145 (bg) Jean and Fred Hort, p145 (ml) Great Ocean Road Coast Committee, p147 (bg) Samuel Frankel, p147 (ml) tjeales, p148 (l) sofiazed1, p150 (br) Norbert Fischer, p151 (ml) J Brew, p152 (ml) Sebastian Doak, p152 (mr) Aggyrolemnoixytes/Paul Marek, p154 (mrb) Cmichel67, p155 (tl) Igor Gvozdovskyy.
Getty Images: p116 (ml) Paul Starosta, p144 (bg) Auscape.
NASA: p154 (br).
Nature Picture Library: p26 (ml), p26 (bl) and p27 (tr) Doug Wechsler, p50 (bg) Stephen Dalton, p51 (bg) Daniel Heuclin, p53 (bl) Mark Moffett, p99 (bg) Kim Taylor, p128 (ml) Nature Production, p135 (br) Jan Hamrsky, p149 (br) Roland Seitre, p155 (br) Doug Allan.
Science Photo Library: p42 (ml) James H. Robinson, p50 (ml) Jerzy Gubernator, p123 (ml) Scott Camazine, p151 (mr) Gregory Dimijian, p155 (tr) British Antarctic Survey, p155 (bl) Theirry Berrod, Mona Lisa Production.

Illustrations by Bethany Lord.